LIVING IN COMPASSION

Living in Compassion

by
Bardor Tulku Rinpoche

translated by
Lama Yeshe Gyamtso
&
Chöjor Radha

Rinchen Publications
Kingston, New York USA

Published by
Rinchen, Inc.
20 John St.
Kingston, NY 12401
Tel: (845) 331-5069
www.rinchen.com

Second Edition, November 2004

Editor: David N. McCarthy
Assistant Editors: Lama Colleen Reed, Drolma Birney, Florence Wetzel
Transcribers: Lama Colleen Reed, Kathi Webster, Tom Vogler,
          Allen Emersonn, & Drolma Birney
Proofreading: Linda Patrik, Richard Thomson, Ilfra Halley, Florence Wetzel
Cover Photos: Ilfra Halley
Cover Design: Sherry Williams/Oxygen Design, Kingston, New York
Printing: Malloy, Inc., Ann Arbor, Michigan

ISBN: 0-97145-540-6

TABLE OF CONTENTS

PREFACE TO THE SECOND EDITION

Living in Compassion first appeared in 2001 and was the first full-length book by the Venerable Bardor Tulku Rinpoche. The book was so well received that a new edition has been needed for some time. I am very pleased and thankful that it is now possible to present a much larger printing of the new edition.

This book is intended as a resource for a broad readership, ranging from those who are new to Buddhist teachings to those who are more experienced. The introduction is a very succinct overview of Buddhism, one that should provide an entryway for those who have had little exposure to the subject. The first section, which presents Rinpoche's views and advice on the subject of marriage and relationships, does so in such a way that it presents a good explanation of the basics of Buddhist ethics, the law of karma, and the vows and disciplines of Buddhism. Rather than delving into elaborate psychological theories of relationships, this section is firmly focused on how we can conduct our personal lives in the context of a Buddhist approach to spiritual practice. This section will be of interest to those with all levels of knowledge and involvement with Buddhism, simply because it touches on some of the most fundamental challenges we face as human beings.

The second and third sections of the book present in-depth explanations of the path of compassion and wisdom, which is the path of the bodhisattva. The second section is a commentary on a 14th-century Tibetan text, *The Thirty-Seven Practices of a Bodhisattva* by Ngülchu Thogme. This is one of the most widely studied texts in Tibetan Buddhism, and is renowned for its simplicity, clarity, and thoroughness.

The third section of the book takes a detailed look at a topic covered briefly in the *Thirty-Seven Practices*, namely the six perfections, or six paramitas. These transcendent qualities are the means by which we actually put the path of compassion into practice in our journey toward enlightenment. Thus *Living in Compassion* brings us from a simple introduction to Buddhism to a clear explanation of the prajnaparamita, the perfection of knowledge.

The colophon of this book is a special section on working for the Dharma and the unique qualities of His Holiness the Gyalwa Karmapa. It was part of the teaching on the six perfections that Rinpoche gave at Karma Triyana Dharmachakra Monastery (KTD) in Woodstock, New York, in the late fall of 1996. The audience was small, and mostly composed of staff and community members associated with the monastery. In preparing the book, I asked Rinpoche if this section should be included, since the book is intended to reach a wider audience than our immediate community. Rinpoche requested that we include it, not only because it is a valuable message to the sangha members associated with KTD nationally and worldwide, but also because His Holiness Ogyen Trinley Dorje, the 17th Karmapa, is now in India. It is only a matter of time before we receive the benefit of his presence in the United States and other parts of the world. Rinpoche feels that everyone—and certainly everyone who is interested in this book—is in a position to receive the blessings of His Holiness the Karmapa and share in his vision and activity.

ACKNOWLEDGEMENTS

I would first like to acknowledge the patience and support of Bardor Tulku Rinpoche himself in the production of this book. This was certainly the case when we published the first edition, and his personal guidance has again been instrumental in gathering the support needed for a substantial second printing. In the years I have known Rinpoche, my appreciation for him has continued to increase, and I can sincerely say that he really does live in compassion. No conceptual explanation can convey the depth of his knowledge and realization, and the degree to which he has generously extended himself to others. However, I hope that many people will come to receive his personal blessings through this book.

I thank Lama Yeshe Gyamtso, who translated the majority of *Living in Compassion*, for his very helpful assistance in the correction of Tibetan and Sanskrit terms, along with clarification of several difficult points in the text. My thanks as well to Chöjor Radha, who translated the first section of the book.

Professor Linda Patrik of Union College in Schenectady, New York deserves a very special expression of gratitude for her help in bringing *Living in Compassion* to print back in 2001. She put her energy and good will behind this project in very helpful ways, including reading through the manuscript completely — most of it more than once — and offering many valuable suggestions and corrections. In addition, she was able to secure grant funding from Union College for the early stages of transcription and editing. I thank Union College for that valuable assistance.

I would also like to gratefully acknowledge the individuals who have provided general financial backing for Rinchen Publications. These include my friend and Dharma brother Cralle Hall, and my mother, Alice R. McCarthy, who has contributed her valuable professional expertise as a publisher as well. I also wish to thank my father and his wife, Walter and Linda McCarthy, for their kind personal and financial support in my Buddhist publishing work.

The printing of this second edition has been made possible with the generous sponsorship of: The Raktrul Foundation, Ann Arbor Karma Thegsum Chöling, Nancy Burks, Jason and Charlotte Flint, David and Beatrice Lin Kendall, Analis and Andrew Quintman, Kirk Moultin, Columbus Karma Thegsum Chöling (with special thanks to Cathy Jackson), and Sue Ellen Steinmetz.

The second edition was enhanced by the work of Florence Wetzel, who reread the entire text and contributed more than a few improvements and corrections. Her excellent editorial work has been a great boon to Rinchen for over a year now. She has worked on many publications, including our most recent book *Rest for the Fortunate*, as well as numerous upcoming titles. I am greatly indebted to her for the ongoing progress and development of Rinchen.

Finally, I would like to make a special note of thanks to someone very dear to me, Ilfra Halley. She is someone whose very real commitment to compassion inspires me greatly. Her personal support, along with her support for the work of Rinchen, has been a tremendous help. Ilfra made a very tangible contribution to this second edition by providing the two excellent photographs that appear on the cover.

Although this work could not have been completed without the help of all these people, I take full responsibility for any errors or shortcomings. My intention has simply been to accurately convey the teachings and intentions of Bardor Tulku Rinpoche. May all who encounter this text give rise to the precious outlook of bodhicitta. And by living in compassion, may we make the best of our human lives.

David N. McCarthy
President, Rinchen Publications
Kingston, New York
October 2004

INTRODUCTION TO BUDDHISM

The teachings of the Buddha are very vast and profound. For us to relate to these teachings, the Buddha did not ask that we accept them merely through faith. In fact, he instructed us to examine the teachings thoroughly for ourselves, and to establish their validity through logical investigation and direct experience. Through examining these teachings and through applying them, it is possible to come to a decisive understanding of the nature of all things. One implication of this is that, from the point of view of Buddhists, Buddhism is not merely a religion. The clarity and understanding that these teachings can bring are applicable to both spiritual and worldly matters. If you think about it, it is clear that the topic of marriage and relationships is one that has both a spiritual and a worldly dimension. This first section of the book will focus on such relationships, both in the context of the traditional teachings of Buddhism, and from a personal and practical point of view.

A Buddhist is defined as someone who is a follower of the Buddha — someone who tries to implement or practice what the Buddha taught. These teachings and practices are referred to as Dharma (or Buddhadharma). Essentially, the practice of Dharma consists of taming or training our minds. The outcome of this practice is to reduce and eventually eliminate the negative psychological patterns of our confused minds. These patterns are known as *kleshas* in Sanskrit, for which there is no exact term in English. *(Editor's note: We will use the translation "mental affliction" for klesha, which is an excellent one as long as it is not understood to mean what is normally meant by mental illness. Kleshas are normal and universal in the sense that all unenlightened beings have them.)* This process of taming the mental afflictions involves working with our behavior and conduct, with how we speak and communicate, as well as with our attitude and state of mind. These three aspects are simply called body, speech, and mind in Buddhist thought.

1

Although Dharma involves working with the body, speech, and mind, in essence the emphasis in these teachings is on the mind. In particular, it is on the internal process of taming our own minds. This fundamentally means abandoning and removing the kleshas — the mental afflictions. Because of this, the term that Buddhists use to refer to themselves — which is perhaps a bit more descriptive than simply the term "Buddhist" — is an "internalist" or, to put it more poetically, an "inner one." This means that the focus is not on attempting to control the external world. The Buddhist emphasis on inner development is based on the view that without an understanding of the mind, our fixation on the apparent solidity and permanence of the external world will only increase our suffering. Therefore what is considered essential to the practice of Dharma is to recognize the nature of our own minds internally. Through doing so, we can come to a proper understanding of what is to be done and what is not to be done.

Doing this internal practice can not be done using conventional or mundane methods. Therefore we make use of the Buddha's teachings — the Buddhadharma. In practicing these teachings we apply the various methods that were taught by the Buddha for overcoming confusion and mental affliction, which make it possible to come to a definite and correct realization of the mind's nature.

Why is it necessary that we work toward taming the mind? It is necessary because the very nature of the mind is insubstantiality or emptiness. Another way of saying this is that our minds are utterly unlimited in their capacity for manifestation. One of the effects of this fact is that if we do not consciously attempt to tame our minds, then our desires will grow endlessly, such that they can never be satisfied. By analogy, if you think about space, it is clearly limitless — it could never be filled. In the same way, our minds' capacity to want or desire is also unlimited. The mind would never ordinarily reach a point where it says, "That's enough, I don't want any more." The reason for this is simply that the

2

nature of the mind can be described as openness, insubstantiality, or emptiness.

There is a traditional saying in Buddhism: "If your control of your physical behavior is excellent, then you will also be able to control your speech. And if you control your physical and verbal behavior, you will naturally be able to control your mind." The saying continues: "The perfect renunciate who in that way controls all behavior of body, speech, and mind will definitely come to be liberated from suffering." The body, speech, and mind are the three faculties through which we function and relate to the world. Because these three are the passageways through which we communicate and express ourselves, they are often called "the three gates." However, the body, speech, and mind also function as the gateways for the development of our mental afflictions, and therefore of negative actions. The fundamental Buddhist discipline therefore consists of abstaining from those actions of body, speech, and mind that are harmful to ourselves and others.

Traditionally it is taught that there are ten basic kinds of non-virtuous actions, and they are categorized in terms of body, speech, and mind. Pertaining to the body, there are three negative physical actions: killing, stealing, and sexual misconduct. Related to speech, there are four negative verbal actions: lying, hurtful speech, slander, and meaningless gossip. Finally, related to mind, there are three mental negative actions: covetousness, spitefulness, and wrong views. Abstaining from these ten actions is what is called the "binding" or controlling of the body, speech, and mind. The result of abstaining from these ten forms of wrongdoing is that we naturally become involved in the ten corresponding forms of virtuous actions, which are the opposites of the negative ones. The outcome of this for ourselves is that we will achieve a state of stable happiness. As well, because we are not actively harming or needlessly disturbing others, then our actions of self-control become a source of benefit and happiness to others. These are the more temporary or immediate benefits. The ultimate benefit of such positive

3

conduct is that we gradually will become liberated from the cycle of suffering (samsara) entirely.

It is definite that happiness and suffering arise from and within our own minds. We can see this clearly by observing our own ordinary world. For example, among all of the countries of this world, America has perhaps the highest standard of living. Nevertheless we still find — in spite of the tremendous prosperity and security we enjoy here — that people do not seem particularly happy. We can see this in more specific ways as well. Who hasn't been to a festive occasion with lots of singing and dancing and laughing, and seen someone there who really has the same reason to celebrate and enjoy themselves as everyone else, but who is totally miserable? This would seem impossible, if it were not for the fact that our state of experience is so subjective. It is really true that a state of happiness or suffering arises within one's own individual mind. Since this is the case, the most important thing to do in the beginning is to gain control over and tame your own mind.

This approach of taking personal responsibility for our own conduct and state of mind forms the basis of Buddhist discipline. Then in the tradition of mahayana Buddhism there is a further breakthrough or expansion of this outlook. Through the clarity and gentleness that arises from taming our own minds, we recognize that all beings are suffering, that they only want happiness, and that they, like us, have the capacity for liberation. With this recognition, we extend our aspiration to the happiness, freedom, and ultimate enlightenment of all beings, not just ourselves.

This vast and profound aspiration forms the basis for the approach of mahayana (which means "the great path"). The method of training the mind in this path involves developing what is known as "bodhicitta." Bodhicitta means the "mind of awakening." Bodhicitta is something that leads to vast amounts of positive karmic accumulation. It is said that if the karmic merit of bodhicitta had form, it would fill the universe and still not be used up. Essentially what is meant by the mind of awakening is the sincere wish that others be happy. It is said that, "The foolish, through attempting to accomplish their own aims, wander in samsara; whereas the wise, in being concerned with the aims of others, attain buddhahood." Although the term "the foolish" sounds quite negative, it really means all of us in the sense that we simply do not understand the truth—we operate under a misconception. In that sense we are foolish. The misconception we operate under is the idea that we can attain some stable state of happiness by attempting to secure our own wealth, our own reputation, our own pleasures, and so on. In fact, by attempting to please only ourselves, we cause ourselves endless trouble. We circle round and round in cyclic existence or samsara. In fact, this has been going on since beginningless time.

Giving up this selfish approach and becoming concerned with benefiting others is the practice of bodhicitta. In realizing that, just like ourselves, all other beings equally wish to be happy and all other beings equally wish to be free from suffering, we will see that accomplishing the happiness of all beings is more important than accomplishing our own. This giving up of concern for oneself, which is bodhicitta, is the cause of becoming a buddha. Therefore it is said that through being concerned with benefiting others, the wise become buddhas. All of this starts with the engendering of bodhicitta, the mind of awakening. Developing bodhicitta is merely a commitment of the mind—it is not the acquisition of something from outside. It is simply a change of attitude. The change consists of no longer being so concerned only with yourself, but being more concerned with others. This is the essence of living in compassion.

What about the personal life and experience of the Buddha himself? How does his life story fit into our discussion of relationships and family in the context of the spiritual path? The Buddha was born as the son of a powerful king whose name was Shuddodhana. As a prince, the Buddha was brought up in a situation of tremendous luxury, and he was raised and trained to succeed his father as the ruler of that

5

region. During the early part of his life, the Buddha actually accepted this situation and his apparent destiny to be a ruler, and he married a queen and had a son. At a certain point in his life, he became dissatisfied with his royal lifestyle. He left worldly life and became a monk. Looking at what he did from the external point of view, from the simple facts, we would say that he was irresponsible or perhaps that he was trying to escape from his obligations. If we were to make that judgement, it would come from only seeing things from an ordinary, conventional point of view. In fact, what the Buddha saw and what made him leave that life of luxury and enjoyment, was the suffering that is inherent in all of existence. In the face of all that suffering, he saw the royal wealth and its attendant lifestyle as futile. He realized that it could not make him or anyone else happy. Therefore, instead of attempting to protect and benefit only those of his region or clan or family, he determined to free all beings. In order to do that, he resolved to attain the ultimate awakening, which would enable him to benefit others in the most effective way. It is for that reason that he gave up his worldly lifestyle and became a renunciate.

Having left the palace, the Buddha did not simply live a carefree life as a vagrant. He practiced meditation under conditions of tremendous austerity for a period of six years. It is said that his austerity went to the extent of, for example, only drinking one drop of water and eating only one pine nut each day. In any case, after these six years of austerity he came to the realization that austerity in and of itself was not enough either. Having thus transcended the extremes of both indulgence and austerity, he went to a place called Bodhgaya, and there, in front of the Bodhi Tree (the Tree of Awakening), he attained full and complete spiritual enlightenment. Having done so he spent the rest of his life teaching. The Buddha's teaching activity is traditionally called "turning the wheel of the Dharma."

MARRIAGE AND RELATIONSHIPS

At the outset, I want to say something personal about this subject: I feel comfortable speaking generally about marriage and the family, and even discussing the shortcomings of such a life, because I myself am married. By contrast, if I were an ordained monk, a celibate person, though I might certainly have valid ideas on the subject, I would not feel as comfortable talking about this, and certainly not talking critically. However, I am not standing outside this way of life. Instead, I am in it, as are most people.

In the various cultures of the world and throughout human history, there have been many different customs and ideas about marriage and relationships. There is really not one single set of standards or views that all societies have had in common. For example, it has been customary in some places for men to have more than one wife. In a few cultures, including some parts of Tibet, a woman could have more than one husband. Despite the fact that there are so many marriage customs — some requiring that a person have only one partner, and some allowing many — by no means have any of these traditions worked out perfectly to produce benefit to couples or families overall.

We can confidently say that there is no particular set of customs or methods that will guarantee having a successful relationship, one that is completely free from any difficulties or problems. It comes down to the fact that you have to make it work. The individuals must make an effort and practice tolerance for one another. Without that, there is really not a formula for success.

Why is this so? Perhaps we need to think about marriage in a more fundamental way than we usually do. From a worldly point of view, we would say that a couple is in a state of suffering when their marriage is going poorly — when there are problems between them, when they do not get along, or when the situation is unworkable in some way. When the relationship goes well and the couple is happy with one another, we would call this a state of happiness. Certainly anyone can see that a couple is suffering when a marriage is not going well, such as when they are always fighting or quarrelling. That is obvious, but really you would have to say there is still going to be suffering when the relationship is a happy one. Even if the couple gets along perfectly, then there are still going to be problems. The children may have illnesses or other difficulties. Even if there are no children, there is always going to be something or another going on. Perhaps the husband will be ill, which will cause the wife worry, or the wife will be ill, which will cause the husband worry. In short, there are continuous problems. It is not as though there are difficulties at one phase of the relationship and not at another. It is simply the way things are.

We also especially need to recognize that the overall situation of a marriage itself is impermanent. It was said by the great siddha Padampa Sangye, "Really a marriage is like two people meeting at a marketplace. You meet to shop, but then you part. The longest time you can possibly expect to spend together is maybe fifty years, maybe sixty, or seventy at the very most, but you are not going to be together for thousands, or even hundreds of years. Thus when you think about the really short duration of a lifetime or marriage, it may make it easier to be kind to one another, and especially to be patient."

There is a text called *The Exposition of the Stages of the Bodhisattva Path* that gives some blunt advice about activities in general. It says, "Don't start something. Once you've started, don't turn back from it." In Asia, it is customary that most marriages are arranged. This can sometimes mean that the couple does not even meet before the day of their wedding, and yet we find there are very few divorces. On

8

the other hand, in the West, marriages are almost invariably by choice. The couple spends quite a bit of time getting to know each other. They enjoy each other and feel attraction in the relationship. They say things like, "Do you love me?", "Do you *really* love me?", and so on. Only after a great deal of negotiation between the prospective husband and wife do they get married. Nevertheless, there is a lot of divorce in the West. The reason there is so much divorce in a situation where you might expect there to be much less, is that there is a lack of understanding of the impermanence and the fleeting quality of the marriage, and also a lack of understanding of the results of actions (karma).

As well, part of the problem is that there is not even a sufficient commitment behind the marriage vows from the beginning. I understand that in marriage ceremonies in this culture, it is common to say things like "for better and for worse," "for richer or poorer," "in sickness and in health." It seems both the husband and the wife say these things, but it is hard to believe they are sincere. It is not so important whether or not such vows are made verbally — it is important they be made mentally. If these vows are really taken seriously, they will really last. For example, when you undertake marriage with someone, you do not do so with the attitude, "Well, I'm willing to marry you now — you are not sick now, you are not poor now, and nothing is ever going to go wrong." In fact, something *will* go wrong. People will become sick, they will go through financial hardships, and they will change. There will be problems, so you have to be aware of that and have a commitment to the marriage that incorporates that awareness from the very beginning. This is another meaning of the saying, "Don't begin something; but once you *have* begun, make sure you finish."

We have to accept the nature of the world as it is. This is traditionally explained by what are called "the four ends." These are: (1) everything that is born will die; (2) every meeting at some point must end in separation; (3) every accumulation must at some point be exhausted; and (4) everything that is created at some point must be destroyed. There is really no exception to this. If we understand and accept this, it will help us a great deal in our relationships and our commitments. The most important thing in understanding the commitment of marriage is to recognize we simply have to finish whatever we start. This is true of things in general — both in the secular sense and in the religious sense. It is highly respected in any culture when we see people who have gotten married and who respect and love one another, and who manage to last their whole lives together. This is commonly praised in the world. It is understood as the point of marriage from a secular point of view.

Looking at marriage from a Dharmic point of view, we need to consider the idea of karma, the law of cause and effect. The general principle of this is that anything you do that is harmful to others will produce future suffering for you, and anything that is beneficial will produce future happiness for you. We could take the action of adultery as an example of karma. Adultery could be primarily motivated by desire or by aggression or by bewilderment. In any case, as the outcome of that activity of adultery, the individual will be born in the future in one of the three lower realms, corresponding to the mental affliction that motivated the adultery. When that karmic accumulation is used up, and the individual is reborn as a human being, he or she will come to have an extremely unpleasant and cruel spouse in that life. These things happen as a natural result of our own previous actions, and because of the traces and habits that these actions ingrain in us which are similar to the action itself. Because these future experiences are the results of our own present actions, we can prevent them simply by not engaging in such actions.

Family Life

Because of their respect for the truth of karma, those who follow the Buddha's teachings are concerned with the results of their actions. Thus the intention to be as helpful as possible to others is the foundation of the Buddhist view on family life. Within this view, there is an attitude of uncompromising love and kindness toward every other member of the family. That is what holds the family together. Essentially what this means is that any suffering that occurs for the family is shared by all. As well, all the happiness that comes to anyone in the family is shared with the others. The idea is that family members give each other as much sharing and help as possible.

Another important principle is the need for contentment — which means accepting what we have and working with it. As long as we have not learned to be content with what we have, as I have said, our desires are limitless. There is a general view in our culture that contentment in a relationship leads to being taken for granted. In reality, being content in a relationship is the basis for being happy. Without this basic peace and acceptance, there is no relief for the mind's constant restlessness and dissatisfaction.

At the same time, the Buddha never said that we can do without alertness. Contentment does not mean complacency. Since we are in samsara, there are many possible ways that people will act out their neurotic patterns and take advantage of us in various ways. We always need to be alert and aware no matter what is happening, but that does not mean that we can not also have peacefulness and acceptance of the situation. We simply need to be wise enough within a relationship such that issues are worked out, and we can avoid being taken for granted or taken advantage of.

The quality of contentment is also necessary in relation to our livelihood, which is obviously very significant for family life. Even if you are quite successful and stable financially and have a good family life, if you were not psychologically satisfied with what you had there would still be a problem. There would always be someone richer than you, or someone that had something you wanted. Without a state of basic acceptance, you are always going to feel jealousy toward others and whatever they have. Again, there is no relief for the mind in that situation.

Another underlying view that is common in our culture is that being at peace about our financial situation leads to poverty. Without having a truly wise view of things, we might come to the conclusion that this is so. What it really means to practice contentment, though, is that whatever you have, you try to learn to be balanced about it and use it beneficially, and develop your financial well-being in a steady way. If you develop your livelihood steadily, without becoming obsessed about material success, but simply work toward your goals with wisdom, that is balance. This brings sanity about how to take care of our families and ourselves. Again, this does not invite us to be complacent. It does not mean ignoring things that are improper or unskillful — either in our own actions or those of others. A work or business situation requires alertness and clear thinking, so the kind of contentment we are discussing here is not inert or dull.

Making correct decisions in life situations requires what is known as discriminating awareness, which is one way of talking about the broader topic of wisdom. As you know, wisdom plays a tremendously important role in Buddhism, and it is clear that we need to apply wisdom in everything we do. In the later sections of the book, we will investigate what is meant by wisdom in the more ultimate, spiritual sense of the word. Here we are discussing the application of wisdom in a practical or worldly sense.

The Buddha made a statement that relates directly to this. He said, "The best wealth is contentment." Using somewhat poetic language, this saying is pointing out the wisdom of accepting what you have. If you are content, you have everything you need. If you are not content, there will be no end to your desires.

Say your goal was to start a lucrative and successful business operation. Even if you succeeded in doing that, you would very likely want to start another one. When you had two, then you would decide that maybe that was not enough. Perhaps you would want to set up another business in another location or another country, and so on. Even though you would be very wealthy at that point, there would be no ease for your mind. Without contentment, the mind can never experience a sense of relaxation and peacefulness. In that case, what is the point of all your wealth? On the other hand, if you learn to be really content, you could be happy even if you were not at all wealthy. Living a simple life, one with sufficient income to provide enough food and clothing, would enable you to maintain a perfectly happy mind. That is what the Buddha meant by, "The best wealth is contentment."

Wisdom is also needed in the skillful handling of what we have. Even if you are quite prosperous, without applying wisdom on an ongoing basis, it is easy to make bad decisions that could lead you to lose that prosperity. As many people have found, being rich at one point does not always mean that you will be successful in the future. And as I have said, it certainly does not insure that you will be happy.

Another way to develop an inner acceptance of relationships is to look at them in terms of karma. The Buddhist outlook is that the particular family or relationship with which we have come to be connected is an outcome of our own actions in previous lives. In the context of a marriage, that viewpoint is a powerful basis for being comfortable with your commitment — of accepting your spouse as he or she is. By taking the attitude that, "I will finish my life with this person whether things go easily or not," then the basic structure of the marriage and of the family is strong. As we have seen, if someone is poor and they possess contentment, then in fact they are richer than a wealthy person, because they are happier. If you lack this attitude in your relationship, such as in a marriage, then you will never be happy no matter what you try to do.

Without contentment, you are at the mercy of your dissatisfaction and desires. The more you allow desire to control your life, the more you will overstep any boundaries you might have set for yourself, and things will get worse and worse. The simple reason for this is, as I have said, that the nature of the mind is empty and insubstantial, and therefore there is no limit to the degree to which desire can grow. Since the mind is in itself nothing whatsoever, it is completely open, and therefore there is no limit to wanting things. For example, at some point in your life you might think, "Well, if I accumulate a million dollars, that will be enough — then I'll be happy." So you accumulate a million dollars and then you think, "Well, that's good, but really I need twenty million." You accumulate twenty million dollars, and then you think, "Well, in addition to that, I need a certain kind of mansion with a certain type of garden and property and this type of car," and so on. It is endless.

If you look at the actions of emperors and dictators, they act the same way with their political conquests. Someone who becomes the ruler of an entire country would think, "Well, this is not enough, I need a second one," so he would conquer another country. Then he would need another one. Since our minds are like space, and space can never be filled, we will never be satisfied by simply getting what we want. If you let desire run your life, there will never come a day when you will feel completely satisfied. That is why the basic approach that is taken in Buddhist spiritual practice, which is also the approach recommended with respect to family life, is to tame your own mind. This is equally necessary whether you are an ordained or a married practitioner.

Some people have the idea that the practice of Dharma and the taming of the mind can only be done in a monastic setting by practitioners who lead intensive lives of secluded meditation. Such people may think, "Well, those of us who are worldly people cannot really practice and get much out of it." From one point of view, there is some validity to the idea that the monastic lifestyle is ideal for practice in the sense that monastics have fewer responsibilities. It is true that they do not have children, and they do not have homes. From another point of view, however, the situation of having a family is perhaps the greatest possible opportunity for genuine Dharma practice. The reason for this is that Dharma practice really consists of the cultivation of the six perfections, namely generosity, morality, patience, diligence, meditation, and knowledge.

We will go over these six perfections in considerable detail in later chapters, but for now, let's briefly consider patience. The best possible opportunity for the development of patience is a family situation. In a family, the husband and wife have an opportunity to develop patience in their relationship with each other. And as everybody knows, children are a huge opportunity for the parents to develop patience! As well, kids need to be taught patience with other children, and they need to learn it for their parents as well. Clearly a family is the best possible opportunity for the cultivation of this quality, simply because patience can only be cultivated in a situation where there is some sort of challenge — something that might make us upset or angry. The essence of patience is really forgiveness. Without someone to forgive, you cannot exercise and develop patience. Therefore in a family, where forgiveness is constantly necessary, we have the best possible opportunity to cultivate patience.

Admittedly, the difficulty of practicing patience can vary quite a lot. According to the truth of karma, the type of marriage situation in which we find ourselves is fundamentally an outcome of our actions in previous lives. Therefore you may find yourself in a marriage that is extremely harmonious and loving. On the other hand, it may be quite quarrelsome—the husband and wife may have strong negative feelings toward each other. Nevertheless, you have to accept the fact that you have ended up with a particular partner as a result of your own previous actions. If you take the attitude that "my relationship with my partner is what it is because of my own karmic accumulation produced by my own previous actions," then you will be able to see that although your partner may presently appear to be hot-tempered, it is not really all coming from him or her. You must have accumulated in previous lives the causes of your partner acting in that way toward you in this life. One karmic cause for having a spouse who is easily angered is having committed adultery in other marriages in previous lives. If you accept your part in this, and also dedicate the situation to the purification of similar sufferings of all beings everywhere, and aspire that the karma that you accumulated in previous lives be purified, then it can be purified. As this karma is purified, then your perception of the marriage and your perception of your partner will change, even down to your perception of his or her physical appearance. It will certainly change how you react to your partner, who you had previously considered so aggressive.

Without seeing things this way, if you take the attitude that any problem in the marriage is the fault of the other person, the whole relationship is threatened whenever problems come up. The man may consider leaving his wife as soon as some conflict appears. He will think, "I need a wife who is nicer, preferably prettier—and certainly richer." It is possible, of course, that he may find a better wife. Probably, though, because of his attitude, he will find a worse one, and if he leaves her, a worse one after that. The basic point of all this is simply that we need to accept and work with our own karma.

Fundamentally it comes down to the fact that since we are in samsara, we all possess the mental afflictions of attachment, aversion, pride, bewilderment, and jealously. We are not enlightened beings, so we have to accept the fact that whoever we marry is going to have the same mental afflictions as we do. If you think that you are going to find a partner who is completely perfect, that is a very naïve attitude. You will never find such a person. Along with that, the things you have done in previous lives are still functioning within you. For example, if you did things in previous lives that caused you to be reborn in the three lower realms, and you then exhausted that karmic accumulation and have now been reborn as a human being, there are still residual results that are functioning in your present life. These are usually called "results concordant with the causes." These residual results would include such things as having problems with your spouse in this life. The Buddhist approach is that if you can purify these tendencies and residual karma in this life, then you will be happy throughout your future lives. If you do not, and if you continue the patterns that maintain this type of karma, then you will certainly accumulate more and more of the causes of similar states of suffering in the future. Your suffering will never end.

Whether you look at it from a spiritual or secular point of view, it is very important to finish what you start. Someone who finishes whatever they undertake is considered a success in the world. He or she is respected and considered trustworthy. For example, if you take on the job of building a house for someone, and you construct it right up from the raw foundation all the way to putting the carpeting on the floor so they can move in, that is respected. It is considered a job well done, and it brings financial well-being and a good reputation. In spiritual development, it is important to finish what you start as well. The basic point here is that if you work out your own karmic patterns, pay attention to the results of your actions, and finish what you have committed yourself to, then things will get better and better as time goes on.

I hope everyone who reads this will take this point to heart. By taking responsibility for your own spiritual challenges — your shortcomings, habitual patterns, and your karmic accumulation from the past — you will bring yourself spiritual and worldly benefit. Not only that, you will also create the basic foundation for harmony in the family, which creates the basis for happiness in future lives for all concerned.

We can look at happiness from two perspectives — temporary and ultimate. Temporary happiness is based on the conditioned circumstances of our mundane experience. For example, if you have a bad headache and take a painkiller, it relieves the pain temporarily. That is a literal example of temporary happiness. There is no guarantee that you will not get another headache in the future. In the same way, if you are suffering from the summer heat and then go into an air-conditioned room, you will also feel temporary relief. As soon as you go back outside, though, you will feel the heat again.

We engage in many activities that we believe bring happiness. This happiness turns out to be merely temporary happiness, which is based on satisfying our attachments and other mental afflictions. Until they are uprooted completely, there is no exhaustion of these patterns. The mental afflictions are like perennials — flowers that bloom every year. Even if you cut the flowers, at the same time the next year more flowers will blossom from the same root. In order to prevent this, you need to tear out the roots of the plant. Usually we take the attitude that by satisfying our desires such as passion, anger, and other kleshas, somehow the strength of these patterns will weaken. However, like the example of the perennial flowers, they continue to return and grow. The only solution is to uproot the mental afflictions in a fundamental way.

How is it that we can uproot these patterns? Attachment, aggression, and ignorance are the primary kleshas we have discussed, but the root of all these main kleshas and their many branches is ego fixation. In samsara, the mind fixates very strongly on the belief of a true, solid existence of self or ego. Based on that entrenched assumption of the existence of self, we then create separation or duality, since by believing in the self we also have to believe in the existence of other. Thus the duality of self and other is inevitably created by the belief in, and fixation on, the self.

Unless we are prepared to discipline our own body, speech, and mind and to apply the discipline in a balanced way in life situations, there is not much of a chance of being free from difficulties or problems in a relationship. The best situation is for both partners to apply themselves sincerely to such practice, working in cooperation with each other. In that case, both of you would clearly understand and accept that you each want peace of mind and freedom from conflicts and emotional pain. The kind of serious, intense quarrels that happen in relationships are actually due to a lack of such discipline and understanding. Those who have been well trained by engaging in the proper discipline can avoid the sort of extreme conflicts and upheavals that destroy relationships. Because of the importance of discipline, we will discuss it in some depth in the next section, and look at the different aspects of discipline that are presented in the Buddhist teachings.

The Path of Liberation

The basic situation we find ourselves in as unenlightened beings is that we are caught up in duality of self and other. You might wonder what the problem is with that. The problem is this: out of that duality, the kleshas naturally develop, such as attachment to those you like, and anger toward those you dislike. Once there is this separation of self and other, the "other" is divided into friend and foe, which brings about all sorts of emotional patterns. All this gets churned up by the fixation on the reality of the self.

Because of this, the Buddha presented three broad categories of discipline: the path of individual liberation, the compassionate path of the bodhisattva, and the discipline of vajrayana. All these are intended to help us develop a discipline of body, speech, and mind. Discipline does not mean being totally rigid or passive. It means that by thinking clearly, you come to understand what is right and wrong, what is helpful and harmful — to others as well as to yourself. Then having that understanding, you abstain from whatever is harmful to yourself and others. Refraining from what is harmful in this way, whether it is physically, verbally, or mentally harmful, is what constitutes discipline.

Among the many types of teaching the Buddha gave, one of the main categories is known as the *vinaya*, which literally means "taming." These teachings are particularly concerned with how to overcome desire and attachment. The essence of these teachings on taming the mind is in the Buddha's discourse known as the *Pratimoksha Sutra*, which means *The Discourse on Individual Liberation*. Just before the Buddha died he said, "I'm passing away now, but this sutra is your teacher from now on; respect it and make use of it." In that statement, the Buddha indicated the importance of applying these teachings on taming the body, speech, and mind. These teachings present three types of lifestyles for Buddhist practitioners. Two of these are for monastics (those who renounce ordinary worldly life) and the other is for a householder or layperson. Since each of these is applicable for men and women, there are a total six lifestyles presented: male and female monks, male and female novices, and male and female householders.

We might ask what actual use these teachings have. The benefit of the four monastic lifestyles is that in such a situation, you are free from the upheaval and responsibility of family life. You are therefore able to concentrate entirely on the activities of meditation, study, and teaching. If you can maintain the lifestyle of a monastic properly, you are assured a virtuous life that is free from accumulating the causes of suffering for yourself, and also you will not cause or enable the cause of suffering for others. In cases where individuals do not wish to be a monastic, or for some reason cannot be a monastic, the lifestyle recommended is that of a *upasaka*, or householder. Householders follow a simpler and more flexible set of vows. Instead of practicing celibacy, they take on the commitment of being faithful to their spouses — in other words to abandon adultery. Although this does not represent a complete transcendence of attachment, it nevertheless means that they are avoiding causing harm and disruption to others with their sexuality.

To explain the lay precepts in more detail, they actually consist of five vows, and to take this form of ordination you can take any one, or any combination of the vows, up to all five. The five are: (1) not committing adultery; (2) not killing a human being; (3) not lying (this refers primarily to lies about spiritual matters, which means such things as making false claims about spiritual experiences or attainment); (4) not stealing; and (5) not indulging in intoxicants. You can take any number of precepts that you think you are ready for and to which you believe you can make a commitment. It is not required that you take all the vows.

The theme of the need for discipline to remedy attachment runs strongly through the teachings of the great Buddhist teachers in history. For example, Nagarjuna said, "It is desire that destroys us, and it is desire that causes us to destroy others." Nagarjuna is not merely referring to sexual desire here. He is referring to desire for anything — for wealth, power, and so on. Desire, when not controlled by some kind of moral discipline, is like a poisonous fruit. You eat it, and you become sick; you give it to someone else, and they become sick as well. I can absolutely guarantee that to the extent you let your desire run wild, you will be in a state of suffering. Part of what maintains our addiction to desire is the mistaken assumption that only desire protects us from apathy. In fact, the absence of desire is not apathy — it is happiness.

Our neurotic behavior is like scratching a rash. When you are doing it there is a sense of pleasure or relief, but the more you scratch it, the more damage you do to your skin. Still there is a strong tendency to do so, despite the fact that you are aware of the damage to your skin, because there is

21

a pleasurable feeling. If we indulge in it, there really is no end to neurotic pleasure.

As a remedy for this, in *The Sutra of Discipline* the Buddha explains the tremendous virtue of undertaking and maintaining discipline. For example, if someone has taken the full ordination of a monk or nun, and is able to purely maintain those commitments, then the virtue of that purity alone—not even including practices such as meditation— would be sufficient to gradually lead that person to enlightenment. This is due to the tremendous accumulation of merit that comes from maintaining the strictness and purity of the discipline. If you understand that, you will come to see that there is a tremendous value in taking on and maintaining the disciplines and commitments that are appropriate for you individually. In and of itself, discipline is of great benefit for spiritual development.

The sutras in general frequently emphasize the value and importance of discipline, particularly that of fully ordained monks and nuns. In *The Samadhiraja Sutra*, it is mentioned that even if someone is able to take on the discipline of complete celibacy for one whole day—twenty-four hours—there is a tremendous virtue in being able to keep that commitment. It goes on to say that keeping such a commitment for a longer period of time multiplies the accumulation of merit accordingly.

In Nagarjuna's *Letter to a Friend,* he said that discipline is like the basis or ground of all good qualities. Just as many things can grow up when there is good soil, when you have disciplined yourself well, all the rest of the enlightened qualities and energies grow out of the goodness of that discipline. If there is no ground or earth, nothing can be grown.

Personally I have a great deal of respect for the celibate monastic tradition. One benefit of this tradition is the matter of personal independence. Especially in the present-day world, we dislike being under the control of others. Since we enjoy having as much independence as possible, the obvious and best solution to having complete independence is simply to be alone. This applies both to men and women equally. Being celibate creates independence. Once you are married, you have to adjust your life and you are not completely independent. You are, to some degree, under the control of another. That being the case, there will be some difficulty in finding time for spiritual practice because you have to adjust to the needs of your partner, not to mention your children. Realistically speaking, having a partner does take time from one's practice, and decreases one's independence.

There are many other reasons for my deep respect for the monastic tradition of full ordination and celibacy. The Buddha himself chose that lifestyle. Being an individual of such great knowledge and wisdom, he must have seen that there was a particular purpose and reason for choosing such an approach. Another great example of this was His Holiness the 16th Karmapa, who followed the monastic discipline with great purity and strictness. In addition to practicing in that way himself, he always encouraged those around him to uphold their vows. Since I grew up with His Holiness as an example, the monastic tradition has inspired me greatly. I would also like to mention that the previous incarnation of Bardor Tulku Rinpoche also set an example of very pure, strict discipline within the monastic life. These influences and background have led me to have a great appreciation of monasticism.

However, we are now in a different kind of time and circumstance. In my present life, due to various reasons and karmic causes and effects, I have followed a slightly different direction than that of the previous Bardor Tulku Rinpoche. I am not complaining about that! I am simply giving you some background, such that you will not come to the conclusion that just because I am married in my present life, I am not in favor of the monastic life or the vow of celibacy. In fact, I always pray that in the future I will be able to follow the Buddha's teaching in a complete way, which was exemplified by Buddha Shakyamuni himself, as well as by His Holiness the 16th Karmapa.

In the Buddhist tradition, we view prayer as being connected with aspiration and motivation, which in turn are connected with our karma. By praying to follow the very footsteps of Shakyamuni Buddha and of His Holiness the Karmapa, I am forming a karmic condition or pattern. Such karmic patterns will eventually lead to the actualization of that aspiration.

How does that karmic formation occur in our actual experience? It is taught in the Dharma that all phenomena, all experiences, are like dreams. For example, say you are having a nightmare, and you wake up from that and you realize you were having a dream. Then you lie there and calm yourself, and try not to think about the nightmare. You think about other things and try to get back to sleep. When you do go back to sleep, you will probably not continue with the same nightmare, though of course you may have another dream. That next dream is really connected to what you had been thinking while lying awake, or perhaps it arose from something you had done in the past or what you might do in the future. In any case, what you experience in the dream is connected to the activity of your mind. Actually, all that we experience in the waking state is like a dream as well. Thus the prayer or aspiration I have made can result in another dream experience in the future, one of following the example of the great enlightened beings in monastic life.

As we have seen, the teachings of the Buddha continuously praise the discipline that is dedicated to overcoming the three kleshas of passion, aggression, and ignorance. In order to overcome these very powerful patterns, the Buddha gave three main categories of teachings which are connected with eliminating these patterns: the vinaya, the sutras, and the abhidharma teachings. Since the vinaya teachings are concerned with overcoming attachment, there is great emphasis on avoiding indulgence through strict rules of conduct.

For those of us who are living in the world, we need to work out a balance between spiritual and worldly life. We can do this by applying the levels of discipline that are suitable for us individually. The Buddha has made three basic types or levels of discipline available to practitioners who are householders. First there are the lay vows, which are part of the individual liberation tradition as taught in the vinaya. This path is also called the *shravakayana*, and the emphasis is on the discipline of physical conduct and activities. Then there is the discipline of the bodhisattva path, which emphasizes training the mind. Finally there are the vows of the tantric path, which are also called *samayas*. It is possible for one person to undertake all three of these disciplines if he or she has the opportunity to receive them and develops the proper understanding. Physically one can maintain the disciplines of the shravakayana, and mentally the bodhisattva path, and then also maintain their tantric samaya.

We should remember that all these vows are based on the basic vow of refuge in the Buddha, Dharma, and Sangha. This is called "taking refuge." I will not discuss it here, because it has been explained so frequently in other teachings and books. However, if you do not know about taking refuge, you should understand that it is the first formal step on the Buddhist path, and that it is a prerequisite for taking any of the other vows we will be discussing.

The Buddha explained the importance of undertaking the three disciplines on the spiritual path by means of an example. He said that without any training in meditation, your mind is like a wild horse. If you try to ride such a horse without a saddle and bridle, you will be in great danger of falling because the horse will not listen to your commands. Once you have trained the horse, and once you have a saddle and so on, you can control the horse and go wherever you wish. Likewise, the Buddha explains that the discipline — particularly that of the vinaya — is of utmost importance towards pacifying and training our wild minds. Once trained, the mind will relate well with the commands, so to speak, of the spiritual path.

25

In this section of the book we have been discussing mostly the shravakayana or individual liberation aspect of Buddhism, and we will also look at the bodhisattva attitude in relationships. Then we will go over the bodhisattva path in some depth in the final two sections. The tantric path will not be discussed in any detail, though you should understand that this is an integral part of the Dharma, one that is strongly emphasized in Tibetan Buddhism. All these disciplines were made available by the Buddha for the purpose of training our minds.

The shravakayana is called the path of individual liberation because it is concerned with taking steps to liberate oneself from samsara. The motivation of this discipline is based on recognizing the meaninglessness and terrible suffering of being entrapped in cyclic existence. Being frightened and concerned by the endlessness of samsaric pain and suffering, we are motivated to liberate ourselves completely from such a situation. Thus we are willing to apply the strict discipline of wholesome and proper behavior. That is the shravaka view. It involves avoiding any harmful activities from the three gates (body, speech, and mind) and engaging in positive, beneficial actions.

As was mentioned earlier, these activities of body, speech, and mind are categorized into ten specific negative actions to be avoided, and they each have a corresponding positive action that is to be practiced. For example, one of the negative actions connected with speech is known as "hurtful speech." This could mean any kind of aggressive verbal abuse, and it could mean creating disharmony between friends, relatives, husbands and wives, or in a community, all by engaging in negative talk. The opposite, positive action would be to engage in gentle, conciliatory, and helpful speech. In a similar way, all ten of the negative actions have opposite positive actions . By refraining from the negative activities of the body, speech, and mind, you will then naturally engage in the ten corresponding positive activities. The practice of abandoning what is negative and taking up what is positive is the essence of discipline, which is called *shila* in Sanskrit. It means having a strong commitment and determination not to engage in any of those harmful activities and to engage in the ten wholesome activities.

It is possible to get a mistaken impression from reading or hearing about the vinaya and the tradition of individual liberation. You may think that unless you take the celibacy vow of a monk or a nun, it is not possible to engage in the vinaya discipline or tradition at all. That is incorrect. The vinaya teaching is actually a flexible discipline for all types of practitioners, whether they are laypeople or fully ordained. Though it is indeed possible to practice this tradition as a fully ordained monk or nun (meaning you have a vow of complete celibacy), there is also the level of novice monastic ordination called *getsul*. This is a discipline that is in-between that of fully ordained monks and laypeople. As well, if you take the lay precepts you are also practicing the vinaya teachings. What it really means to practice the vinaya is to maintain a strict discipline of refraining from the ten unwholesome activities of the body, speech and mind, and of mindfully engaging in the ten wholesome activities. That itself really could be called the tradition of individual liberation. In essence, there is no other practice or discipline of individual liberation other than that.

One example of practicing the essence and simplicity of the teachings is this: in ancient times, there were many people whose kleshas were not so powerful as they are now, and their wisdom was sharper because they had fewer mental obscurations. Practitioners such as these, who knew and applied the simple summary of the Buddha's teaching which says, "Do not commit any evil whatsoever; practice virtue completely; pacify your mind," could obtain liberation. These lines express the essence of the Buddha's teaching, and because people's minds were clearer and calmer then and their neurotic patterns were not as strong, they could practice and achieve the result based on that teaching alone.

In today's world our neurotic patterns are much stronger. Because of that, and although wisdom still is present within us, our mental obscurations are very thick. We are unable to understand and implement something that simple and direct, and therefore we need a more powerful discipline and teaching. We could make an analogy between kleshas and spiritual discipline, and sickness and medicine. If the sickness is a very minor one, the medicine that needs to be applied does not have to be very powerful. If the disease is very powerful, you will need to apply an equally powerful remedy to overcome that disease. Since our mental afflictions have become more powerful and coarse, we now need to apply a more powerful remedy which is a very strong, strict, and comprehensive discipline.

Based on the skill, compassion, and wisdom of the Buddha, he has consistently provided us with the proper disciplines for our needs. We can make our own choices about which of these are best. If an individual chooses to engage in the discipline of being a fully ordained monk or nun, then that strong and complete discipline is available. If someone does not want to become a fully ordained monk or nun, yet does not want to be a householder, the *getsul* vows can be taken by both men and women. Then there is the *upasaka* vow which allows those who choose to have a family and to live in the world to practice the vinaya as well. Then there are practitioners who have no wish to take a long-term vow, and the Buddha did not exclude them from his teachings either. There are short-term practices such as the *nyinay* and the *nyungne* in which you can take certain sets of vows for one or two days. Usually these are done in a meditation retreat situation.

With all this in mind, we should not get discouraged and think that the Buddha did not provide the disciplines of individual liberation to lay practitioners. Indeed he did provide such disciplines for us. We just need to develop a sense of trust in the Buddha's teachings and in ourselves. Knowing the disciplines that are available, it is then your own responsibility to take on whatever level of discipline is appropriate, based on your lifestyle and self-understanding.

All of these types of discipline, and the vows that go with them, are connected with having knowledge and respect for cause and effect, or karma. It is taught that nothing can happen without a cause. That is true even in the case of being born as a human being. For us to have been born as a human being in this life, there must have been a cause, and if we are to have a human birth in the future, there has to be a cause for that. Just because we are a human being now does not mean that we will be a human being again in the next life. If that is to happen, it is necessary to create the cause for that ourselves. Buddhism teaches that there are six realms of existence. The realm in which we take birth is based on our accumulation of karma. Normally the realms of the gods, demi-gods, and humans are regarded as the higher states of birth compared to the other three. They are not enlightened realms, but they are superior to the lower realms (animals, hungry ghosts, and hell beings).

Out of all the six realms, our human realm provides the greatest opportunity to progress toward enlightenment. Since the greatest opportunity exists here, it is appropriate to try to create the cause that will again lead us to experience birth in the human realm. The cause that is necessary for that is a strong practice of discipline. If you are lacking in strong discipline, the possibility of rebirth in the human realm is quite remote. Creating the cause for such rebirth does not mean you have to become a fully ordained monk or nun. It can also come about by undertaking any of the vows and disciplines we have been talking about — whether it is the novice ordination, lay precepts, or the temporary vows. By practicing in this way, we can create and maintain the causal conditions for human rebirth, which is so important for our spiritual practice and eventual enlightenment. Buddha Shakyamuni himself said that he could not just magically bring us into a state of enlightenment, but that he could provide us with the techniques or methods to get there. Having been provided with the methods for progress on the path, we then have to put our own effort into the process.

It is traditionally taught that there are five conditions, which are known as the five certainties, that are necessary to properly receive any of the different kinds of vows that we have been discussing, such that we can really practice the discipline very effectively.

The first is the "certainty of location." This means taking the attitude that you will maintain the vow under all circumstances, not just when things are easy and convenient. Regardless of where you are, in whatever environment and under whatever conditions, you commit to upholding the vow you have taken.

The second certainty is "certainty of time." For whatever vow you take, this means taking it for the appropriate time frame that goes with the vow. For example, if you are taking full monastic ordination, you do not think, "I'll take this for just a week, a month, or a year." Instead, you take the vow intending to uphold it completely for the rest of your life.

The third certainty is the "certainty of life." This means not taking the vows with the thought, "I'll keep these vows as long as I'm not in danger; if my life is in danger, then I'll give them up." Instead the vows should be taken with the attitude that you will always preserve and maintain them, whether you are in danger or not.

The fourth of these is known as the "certainty of persons." This means that you must not limit your intention to thinking that, "I'll practice wholesome actions and avoid harmful actions only towards people that I like; if someone really hurts or harms me, or if it is someone that I hate, then I will not practice this for them." In doing that, you are separating out certain beings for whom you will not keep the vow. This is to be avoided in taking on commitments or disciplines correctly.

The fifth certainty is literally called the "certainty of the branches," and it means upholding the completeness of the vows you take. The main vows of any ordination are called root vows, and then there are more minor vows, which are called branch vows. Whatever type or level of vows you take, you must take them in a serious and complete way. You should not think, "Well, some of these vows are very difficult, so maybe I'll skip those." You should not evaluate the vows, thinking certain ones are important and others are not. If you view particular branches as unimportant, this is your own judgement as to what the branches should be, which indicates a lack of certainty. Whatever vows you take, the appropriate way to take them is to take them on in a complete way, regardless of whether you think they are important or unimportant, hard or easy.

When you are able to accept the vows in their complete form and discipline yourself accordingly, that will lead you to experience what is called the sacred, ultimate bliss. That bliss is indeed the ultimate and sacred relationship or marriage. There can be no better relationship than that.

Discipline and the Understanding of Karma

In the ordinary world, it is very common for married couples — no matter what their nationality — to be constantly arguing with each other and having problems due to differing viewpoints. The emotional upset that these arguments create brings a great deal of suffering, and makes resolving whatever real issues might exist even harder. The real reason behind such arguments is a lack of discipline. Because of the lack of discipline, both partners are constantly getting carried away with their selfish attitudes. By a selfish attitude here, I mean the stubborn wish that your spouse or family members will do exactly what you want them to do. This kind of attitude brings about a deep disharmony. If the mind is disciplined — which means going beyond selfishness toward a deeper understanding of all concerned —

then there is a prospect of developing a whole new tone to the relationship. Therefore when I talk about developing the discipline of observing vows, particularly the lay precepts, I am not just talking about the prospect of spiritual development from that. The outcome and benefit of such a discipline holds the very real possibility of worldly happiness as well, in the sense of creating a better relationship between partners.

Another thing that is essential for a good relationship or marriage is the understanding of karma. As humans, we have taken birth in what is known as the desire realm of samsara. This means that we have craving and attachment for wealth, possessions, and sensual pleasure, and thus we are subject to mental afflictions such as desire, anger, and so on. As I have said, if unchecked, these patterns are really limitless. Though the wisdom aspect of our mind is always present, the mental afflictions block or obscure this wisdom, which prevents us from being able to see situations in their depth and clarity. When we first meet someone to whom we are sexually attracted, there is a great deal of passion. Under the sway of desire, we experience a superficial reality at best. We simply believe what we see on the surface, which is fundamentally deceptive. We often fail to recognize the person's actual personality. If the person is physically or mentally ill, we also fail to see that due to our passion. Because of our samsaric patterns, the process of getting involved with someone and conducting that relationship over time is fraught with uncertainties. Understanding karma, however, can bring some perspective that we ordinarily do not have.

It is said if you want to know how you acted in a past life, look at how you are now. If you are doing well, are mentally and physically healthy, and are in good circumstances, that means you have done good things in your past life. You can apply that basic perspective in understanding others as well. By understanding karma, you will come to see that it is due to positive actions in the past that you now have a human birth. This is something we need to appreciate. Also, as you grow in your knowledge of karma, you will naturally be inclined to behave in ways that build up an increasingly positive karmic accumulation.

In Tibet, because of the strength of Buddhism in the culture, and the respect for karma that goes with that, it takes quite a while before a couple really commits to getting married. There is serious consultation, not only with the parents of the two persons who want to get married, but also with high lamas and teachers. They also normally consult with an astrologer. Whether the marriage should take place or not depends on the indications from all these sources.

The custom of consulting lamas and astrologers is based on the acceptance and recognition of karma in relation to marriage. In traditional Tibetan culture, it is very rare that a marriage does not go well. This does not mean that Tibetan couples do not have problems — they do. However, because they have consulted so many respected authorities, they tend to take the view that they are not going to find someone better, so it is best to work out those problems.

A real understanding of karma also teaches us to have tolerance, which is so essential in making a marriage work. Ordinarily, we tend to blame each other whenever there is a problem. Often the reason behind separation is a simple lack of tolerance in the relationship. The fact is that problems will exist no matter who you are married to. The proper understanding of karma would be that negative things happen to us due to *our own* negative karma. Understanding this creates a whole different basis for partners to have acceptance and tolerance for each other.

When the partners have a strong understanding of karma, the relationship could develop in a very wholesome and positive direction. You would see the importance of not taking your partner for granted, and not being deceptive with him or her. You would really see that having love and caring for each other is the true, authentic way to be together.

Seeing things in that way is to see a deeper purpose for the relationship.

Without that understanding, in most cases a relationship is really just a matter of attraction and infatuation, and the self-deception that goes with that. At the beginning when you are strongly attracted to the person, you see all his or her good qualities. You idealize the person and think they have no faults at all. Everything seems perfect, but then after you have been together for a while, perhaps a few years, then you see all the opposite things. Nothing seems right; everything seems to be wrong with this person. It is almost like it is not the same person. How can that be possible? Has the person really changed all that much? Actually what has changed is your perception. That is the indication that you have been deceived by attraction and infatuation at the beginning of the relationship.

If you had a clear understanding of karma, you could work with this in a better way. I am still talking about a quite ordinary relationship here. You would still go through the basic pattern of a "honeymoon" phase at the beginning where things seem very rosy, and then eventually encounter some problems and see each other's basic negative patterns. People without a deeper understanding will often begin disliking their partner as soon as a problem comes up. Unable to have the slightest patience or tolerance for their partner, it seems like the best thing to do is start looking for a new one. But as I have said, in samsara there is really no such thing as a perfect match. You will always run into various kinds of problems no matter how many times you change partners. Practitioners of Dharma would recognize that regardless of who we find, samsara is filled with faults—including their own. Knowing that fact, and despite the problems in a relationship, they would try to be tolerant of each other and resolve those problems. They would communicate sincerely and try to meet each other halfway and come to an understanding of each other.

Obviously I am not saying that any relationship can be resolved or that you have to stay together at any cost. For example, that is certainly not the case where the anger and abuse are such that you are in fear for your physical safety. At the same time, if one or both of the partners are not totally happy as the relationship goes on, that is not always a reason to split up. Of course, this always depends on the specific situation. But the Buddhist view would be that an understanding of karma is something that extends beyond this life. It is said that whatever you can complete in this lifetime, you will be able to complete in the next lifetime as well. Conversely, our inability to complete something in this lifetime is also a result of our not having done so in a past life. Thus if we are unable to complete the commitments of a marriage or relationship in this life, and go through a pattern of constantly changing partners, we will experience the same pattern in the next life as well. With that knowledge, unless the situation is quite hopeless, those who understand karma would try to develop more tolerance and work toward resolution.

With marriage, there is the possibility of making some sacrifice in this life to really work out your karmic pattern concerning relationships, which will then positively affect your future lives. If a marriage is not perfect, but the partners try to stay together and fulfill that commitment, there can be benefit in that. Though they are not perfectly happy, they are not creating some sort of negative karma by staying together. In fact, since they are fulfilling the commitment of marriage in this lifetime, they are creating a karmic pattern of fulfillment for the next life. In the next life they will have no problem with success in marriage, and other things as well. That is a basic point of karma and its result: that instead of being just concerned with our present life, we can work with the patterns that affect all our future lives.

Understanding karma is essential in relation to your children as well. The Buddhist view is that your children have a karmic connection with you based on a previous life. As a result of that, they are with you in this life. This Dharmic view would only reinforce the normal, healthy attitude of parents that we should dedicate our utmost care and love for the betterment of the child and for the child's future. Buddhist parents would raise their children with that attitude. However, having done their best for the child's future, the parents would remain open to the kind of person the child turns out to be. After all, that is based on the child's own karma. Your child may well turn out to be quite different than you have wished. Someone who understands karma would not get totally frustrated in that case, and would recognize what is at play. As well, the parents would accept that it is an expression of their own karma if their children turn out differently than they expect. That sort of understanding can completely clear the air in the relationship between parents and children. And if children are brought up understanding the concept of karma, they will accept their parents as they are, just as their parents have accepted them.

One of the great mistakes parents make is trying to force their children to develop in their own image. Of course, this does not mean that Buddhist parents should not discipline and educate their children. Clearly the proper approach as a parent is to be loving and understanding, and to discipline and educate your children in the best way possible. This means avoiding harshness and violence, and trying to instill a sense of understanding in them. With that kind of parenting, you are doing the best that you can. Having done your best, though, if your child goes in a different direction than you may have expected, a Buddhist parent would let the child have the freedom they need to go in their own direction. If we try to mold our children in their career choices, for example, it creates tremendous frustration and negativity within the family. For Buddhist parents, if they treat a child well and provide a good education, then whatever life direction the child chooses — which is based on the child's karma — does not frustrate the parent. This kind of acceptance brings good communication, harmony, and closeness to the relationship between parents and their children.

The Bodhisattva Attitude in Relationships

As I have emphasized throughout this section, the basic Buddhist approach is to resolve problems in relationships, not to escape from them. In order to do that, it is essential that we develop the proper outlook or state of mind. To convey to you the key point about such a proper mental attitude, I would like to conclude this discussion on relationships by explaining the bodhisattva attitude in relationships. This depends on developing and maintaining our bodhicitta, the mind of enlightenment.

In our discussion of karma, we saw that, as Buddhists, we would regard problems and difficulties in a relationship or family as the outcome of our own negative actions in the past, and that by running away from the relationship, we are not going to escape the basic karmic pattern. How could we bring bodhicitta into this situation? We could do so by taking the attitude that, "In undergoing this negative experience, may I take on and remove all such negative experiences of all living beings." Taking on such a vast and compassionate attitude transforms the situation completely, in the sense that we are not simply remaining in our ego fixation and complaining about the situation.

This is very similar to the way that those on the bodhisattva path are taught to look at illness. They think, "May this illness, which is the result of my negative karma, take away the illnesses that all the countless sentient beings are experiencing." Looking at suffering and illness in this way may not get rid of your illness at a physical level, but it can transform your psychological experience. In relationships, such an attitude can help you develop the mental strength and clarity such that the problem can be faced and resolved. By contrast, trying to escape from problems is like trying to run away from your own shadow. No matter how hard you run, it will still be with you.

37

Once you are resolved to overcome your karmic patterns, attachments, obscurations, and so on, the practice of meditation is vital. Meditation reveals and strengthens the wisdom that is present within us. Meditation weakens the kleshas. Although it does not completely eliminate the mental afflictions right away, they are diminished and wisdom becomes more powerful. Then you will not fail to recognize the truth about whatever is going on in your life. At that point your understanding of karma becomes very vivid and direct.

Thus if you seriously want to eliminate the problems you face, you should develop a strong practice of meditation. That is the key. By meditation I do not simply mean the practice of sitting quietly to develop the stability and calmness of the mind. That is essential, of course. In addition to that, the bodhisattva approach to meditation involves developing firm and consistent loving-kindness and sincere compassion. By developing these qualities, there is the real possibility of stable happiness and freedom from problems. Without this attitude, you will never have happiness simply based on finding the right partner, which is usually so involved with our attachments and obscurations.

Normally when we say we love someone, we actually mean we are attached to them. We love someone when they appeal to us and treat us favorably. If not, we develop antipathy and aggression toward them. However, genuine love as defined in Buddhism is not based on attachment. It is the pure attitude of openness, compassion, and wishing well to a person, whether they are your friend or your enemy. It is completely unconditional.

That is the way a bodhisattva loves. This love is described as being "immeasurable," which means that there is no limit to the depth or expanse of that love. It is beyond an ordinary person's imagination. This love is the same whether someone is a friend or an enemy. Just as a mother loves her only child, the bodhisattva loves every living being equally and impartially. The bodhisattva's outlook toward beings is described as "the four immeasurable qualities." These are: the wish that all beings be free from suffering and the causes of suffering, that all beings have happiness and its causes, that beings have the sacred happiness that is beyond suffering, and that they have what is known as "the great equanimity."

With such an immeasurable love, being able to tolerate and overcome problems in a relationship starts to seem a little less daunting. Bodhisattvas have the aspiration to bring all sentient beings to happiness. Of course, your partner or spouse is one of those living beings! If you are willing to compassionately tolerate the negativity of all beings, then to tolerate one person's negativity is nothing in comparison. In this way we learn to have true patience and tolerance for our partners, and a sense of compassion for them about their shortcomings.

It is traditionally taught that bodhisattvas have three kinds of profound tolerance in their journey of benefiting beings. These are called the tolerance of the three conditions. The first is to have tolerance at all times, which means that bodhisattvas have the tremendous tolerance that enables them to work for limitless aeons to benefit beings. The second of these is the tolerance of the number of beings. Beings are as limitless as the sky itself — there is no end to their number, and bodhisattvas are willing to work with all of them. Finally, bodhisattvas can tolerate hardships and difficulties. Because of their wisdom and understanding, the bodhisattva's tolerance or patience is not shaken by any hardships or sufferings they might have to go through to benefit living beings. In summary, bodhisattvas have the courage and fearlessness to not be discouraged by the length of time it takes, or the number of beings there are, or by the difficulties they may encounter as they work to benefit beings.

When you consider the vastness of the bodhisattva's intentions, marriage may not seem like such a big deal! Bodhisattvas take care of limitless beings, but in marriage you are only sharing your life with one person. We might ask why it seems so hard to tolerate the problems that come up with one individual when bodhisattvas tolerate countless individuals. Thus the bodhisattva attitude, both as an example and in actual practice, can bring about a profound tolerance in relationships.

If we make the effort to practice acceptance and tolerance, it is really possible to come to terms with each other and be successful in our relationships. With the bodhisattva attitude, we can make the best use of any difficulty and suffering that come about, rather than creating negative karma out of those situations.

As we close this section, there are a few things I would like you to remember. First, there are a few more thoughts from Padampa Sangye, who was one of the great teachers of Buddhism in Tibet. He said that much of the time our communications with each other are like the way people talk in a crowded marketplace. People are all chattering at the same time but not listening to each other. He was saying that we need to learn to listen to each other, appreciate our relationships, and learn to work with the difficulties of the situation rather than alienating ourselves from each other. He also said that it is the responsibility of men and women to love each other and work out their relationships.

Another thing to remember is a very important teaching given by Shantideva. He said that of all the jewels that you can find in the cosmic universe, the most precious jewel is really contentment. If you learn to have contentment, that is the most valuable thing, because there is happiness in contentment that you cannot get otherwise. Because the nature of samsara is suffering, the situation of a human being in samsara is one of endless craving. If you do not have contentment, you will never reach the end of desire. Since there is no end to the desire, even if you are successful in getting the things you want, you will never be satisfied. Learning to be content does not mean that you have to give up everything. It means coming to appreciate whatever you have. Within that appreciation and contentment, there is happiness.

Finally, we need to remember the fundamental fact that we have the great fortune of having been born as human beings. To obtain a human birth does not happen by accident. It happens due to a tremendous accumulation of merit. Specifically it means that in the past we have engaged in a positive discipline of our body and mind, and we have refrained from harming others. This has also resulted in our present connection with the Dharma. Given that situation, it is important to recognize and appreciate our own good fortune and make some use of it. There is a traditional Buddhist story that tells of a merchant who finds himself on an island filled with priceless jewels — diamonds, gold, and silver. The whole environment there is filled with these precious things. He walks about in amazement and wonder, but when he leaves, he somehow forgets to take any with him. Our birth as human beings could be like that if we do not take advantage of this opportunity to practice the Dharma. I pray and trust that each and every one of you who has made the effort to study this teaching will take this to heart. May you recognize and make use of your human birth and connection with Buddhism, such that you do not end up like the merchant who returns empty-handed from the island of jewels.

Bardor Tulku Rinpoche

QUESTIONS AND ANSWERS

Question: If you are married and your spouse commits adultery, how should you work with that? Do you have to just accept it as your karma or can you work with the situation?

Rinpoche: It is correct to regard it as your own karma if you have been the victim of adultery, and that may help you understand it better and come to terms with it. However, it is not right to use that viewpoint in some sort of fatalistic way to avoid dealing with the situation. It has to be resolved one way or the other.

The point of marriage, after all, is for two people to face life together with a common view that has both of their interests at heart. In that situation, any serious disagreement or any serious conflict that threatens the union of the marriage has to be resolved. It can not simply be swept under the carpet. Minor disagreements in view and so on are normal, and they should not be regarded as reason for separation. But something major such as this has to be worked out.

Question: I was interested in your statement about not beginning something, but once you have done so, to finish it. Could you say a bit more about that?

Rinpoche: What I meant by "better not to begin" is you should not hastily enter into a state of marriage. This means that you should not get married until you are absolutely sure, or reasonably sure, that you want to marry this person and also that this person wants to marry you. Often it can happen that a man will fall in love with a woman and become possessive, and this sexual possessiveness is not uncharacteristic of men. In that situation, he may not carefully examine whether or not the woman really wants to marry him. He may convince her to marry him against her own better instincts. Obviously getting married is something that involves two people, and the wishes of both should be equally clear and strong before doing so.

Question: Say that in a marriage of ten years or so, it comes to the surface that there is a spiritual difference between the partners. This could be a difference in beliefs, or perhaps one partner is growing in a direction they were not aware of when they first got married. Do you feel that a separation is appropriate for spiritual differences like that? If not, how would you stay together?

Rinpoche: It should not be necessary to leave the relationship in that situation, for two reasons. The first is that although a marriage can involve a religious ceremony at its beginning, basically it is not a religious matter, it is secular. You do not get married for the sake of religion, you get married for the sake of love. The love you have for your partner does not have to change because either of you has changed religious orientation. They are still the same person. There may be something new in one of your lives, but fundamentally you are still the same people. There is no reason why you can not love one another just as much. The second thing is an extension of the first. It is always necessary to distinguish between your secular life and your religious life, and not allow one to destroy or interfere with the other. If you have that kind of balance in your life, it should be possible for either spouse to avoid interfering with the religious life of the other. Each should have a basic attitude of sympathy and enthusiasm for whatever the other person does.

Actually a problem with spirituality like this is very likely symptomatic of an inequality of power within the marriage. Usually when one or the other partner is trying to control the other, this issue comes up.

Question: When it comes to maintaining a proper relationship, does it matter if the couple is of the same gender?

Rinpoche: The basic criterion for a good relationship is one of commitment—that each partner is concerned with the welfare of the other. That would apply if they are of the same or different gender.

Question: You said that as ordinary beings, we are going to make mistakes. How does that connect with karma? Once you have committed adultery, for example, are you karmically done for?

Rinpoche: Although we try to do our best, we are not perfect. Until we attain buddhahood, we still have mental afflictions and still make mistakes. But you will make far fewer mistakes and harm others far less if you resolve to do your best, to behave as well as you can, and to be as considerate to others as you can. Then your behavior will definitely be better than if you let yourself go with however you feel at any given moment.

Concerning an action such as adultery, it should be regarded as a serious situation, with serious karmic results. According to Buddhism, however, you should never think that what you have done in the past can not be purified. There is always something you can do about it. A great deal of the methodology in Buddhism consists of ways of cleaning up the damage we have done to ourselves or others from wrongdoing in the past, as well as the ways of expanding or nourishing the virtue we have already cultivated.

Question: We have a serious problem in our society with violence against women in marriage and relationships. What would your advice be concerning physically battered or abused women?

Rinpoche: First of all, being subjected to violence is the clearest possible indication that you should end the relationship and get to a situation of safety. It is definite that you have the wrong partner. This is the kind of extreme situation that hopefully can be avoided by getting wise and insightful guidance before entering into a relationship.

Question: Do you think marriage is necessary for couples who are in a long-term relationship?

Rinpoche: From the Buddhist viewpoint, love and caring are the most important aspects of a relationship between men and women. The whole formal tradition of marriage is not as important. If you get married without having that sense of love and caring for each other, it really does not matter that you are married. The attitude you take toward being together is more important than the fact of being married in itself.

Question: One important quality you have talked about is limitless compassion. Sometimes there are situations, however, where that particular attitude might not be understood. Perhaps someone like a drug addict or an alcoholic may see your compassion and decide to take advantage of you. Do you have any suggestions on how to practice compassion in that situation?

Rinpoche: In walking the bodhisattva path, we need to avoid what has been called "idiot compassion." That refers to compassion that tries to be "nice" and make people happy. It involves doing what they want rather than what is needed. It is really about making ourselves feel good, rather than actually practicing compassion. What is missing in this is wisdom. Bodhisattvas cultivate and practice limitless compassion which is endowed with the quality of wisdom. When you have that, no one can take advantage of you because of the sharpness and clarity of that wisdom. It cuts through any faults or mistakes that might come about, including being taken advantage of. In a situation where someone is trying to take advantage of you, you will actually know what will benefit them and what will not. With that awareness, you can apply your compassion and do your best for that person, even if it means not doing what they want. When the compassion is joined with authentic wisdom in this way, the outcome will always be beneficial.

Bardor Tulku Rinpoche

Question: I am having a lot of difficulty trying to figure out how to have compassion for people who are very hostile or angry or bitter, and I find it is easier if I can understand where the bitterness comes from. I can see that their anger is really a way of expressing the desire to live a more full life, and that they do not know how to do so except through their anger. I am trying to develop some understanding in that way, but I do not really know what to do other than just to stay away from such people. Do you have any comment about the source of such ugliness?

Rinpoche: Their ugliness really comes from a selfish outlook. Actually, both good and bad people have their own kinds of selfishness that they hold on to. Both kinds of people want to have happiness and to be free of suffering. If someone is generally kind, however, that person may desire personal happiness, but his or her attitude does not exclude others. They are aware that others also want to be happy and free from suffering. Thus kind people tend to be helpful and pleasant to deal with. People who are ugly and negative do not maintain the same awareness. They do not understand others. They are preoccupied with their selfish attitude. They fixate on trying to fulfill their own desires, sometimes even to the point of killing, stealing, and harming beings in other cruel ways. This is all based on selfishness.

Question: One area that is often difficult in marriage is financial matters. Based on what you have said, it seems that could arise from the two people having different levels of desire and different levels of contentment with what they have. How do you reconcile your differences of degree of contentment or desire and work it out?

Rinpoche: In general, problems arise due to our stubborn clinging to our own views — in short, because of ego. Therefore couples need to learn how to compromise. Perhaps if you are content with what you have, you can try to be a little more ambitious in order to please the other person. If you are someone who is more ambitious than your partner, then perhaps you can tone down your ambitions. In that way there is cooperation. You need to meet each other midway.

Question: How can two people decide to have children, and what is the appropriate way to raise children? In Tibet, is there any distinction between the role of the father and mother?

Rinpoche: Since there are so many difficulties and problems in our world today, I really cannot advise you in general whether to have a child or how many you should have. Each couple needs to make a decision based on their own understanding and wishes. If you do have a child, it is really the equal responsibility of both the mother and the father to take care of that child, to educate that child well, and to teach the child the difference between right and wrong. They both need to do this with a real sense of love, compassion, and understanding, and without being harsh or violent.

Question: What exactly is meant by sexual misconduct?

Rinpoche: It depends on the precepts or vows that you have taken. If you have taken the particular lay precept against adultery, it means that the husband and wife are committed to being faithful to each other. This means that they will not get involved sexually with anyone but their spouse. Thus in this case, adultery is regarded as sexual misconduct. If you take the vow of complete celibacy, as is done in monastic ordination, then engaging in sex at all would be regarded as sexual misconduct.

Question: From what you have said, I have been getting the idea that maybe the more advanced spiritual beings should be the ones to get married, and the rest of us should just work out our personal discipline and overcome the obscuration of desire.

47

Rinpoche: Well, it is not necessary that the advanced spiritual beings get married. It is said in the teachings that the manifestation and activity of enlightened beings will coincide with whatever will be of benefit to the beings of the time and place where they appear. An enlightened being such as His Holiness the Karmapa, who has gone beyond passion, does not have the desire or craving to have a partner. If there is a need, however, they do get married. For example, the 15th Karmapa was married and there was a reason for that. His son was the second incarnation of Jamgön Kongtrül. Then, after that, the 16th Karmapa once again practiced the vows of celibacy very strictly, so there must be a reason for that as well. Whether such beings lead their lives in celibacy or as a householder is in keeping with whatever is beneficial to beings.

The way that enlightened beings work to benefit others is really beyond our conception or imagination. There are many enlightened beings that manifest in ordinary appearances such as humans, animals, and so forth—even as plants and flowers—all in order to be of benefit. Due to our lack of spiritual development we are not aware of these manifestations.

Such beings also perform profound acts of generosity and sacrifice for others. The 15th Karmapa told a story about one of his own previous lifetimes. It illustrates how enlightened beings manifest in order to pacify and cultivate the seed of virtue and Dharma in certain individuals—beings in whom cultivating that seed would otherwise be almost impossible. There was once a very powerful, cruel king who enjoyed hunting and killing animals. Nothing made him feel any pity or compassion. Therefore the Karmapa manifested in the form of an elephant with six tusks, because the king particularly liked hunting elephants. The elephant approached the king's hunting party in the forest and allowed himself to be killed. Since an elephant with six tusks was considered a very special hunting trophy, the king invited all his attendants to a feast at which they ate the meat of the elephant. Due to the blessing of this enlightened being, whoever ate or even touched the meat gave rise to bodhicitta. That was his intention in manifesting in the form of an elephant. Thus enlightened beings manifest in many different ways, often in various beneficial forms that we are unaware of. When it is appropriate, marriage is one of those ways.

Question: What about a marriage in which there are so many differences and so much negativity you cannot see any wholesomeness in it at all? In situations like that, how does one work within a marriage relationship? I guess I am asking what your notion of grounds for divorce would be.

Rinpoche: Just to give some background, in more ancient times the idea of divorce or separation was largely unheard of in traditional cultures. When it did happen, it was so unusual that the news spread all over the countryside and people would be genuinely shocked to hear about it. Now in the modern world, of course, the concept of separation and divorce is taken quite lightly. Since everyone has accepted it, it is not any kind of a big deal. I feel there are two main reasons that divorce has become so common.

The first reason is that because of the initial physical attraction people have for each other, they do not really think over fully how living together is actually going to be, with all the practical challenges that go with that. They go into marriage sort of blind in that sense, and within some time after being married, things start to change between them. In particular they gradually lose their physical attraction for each other, and the only solution seems to be to separate. This goes back to all the deception and delusion I have mentioned that comes with with infatuation and physical attraction.

The second reason goes back to the point I made about the seriousness of the formal vows we take in getting married. Even though you say words like, "in sickness and in health, for richer or poorer" and even, "until death do us part," the reality behind that is questionable. That much I have already said, but what I want to add is this: what I often see in couples is actually a sense of competitiveness between them — and even jealousy. At some level they are trying to outdo each other and will feel a lot of jealousy about the other's success. In discussions I have had with many men and women it seems that the competitiveness between husband and wife is much stronger than their competition out in the world! When you have such a strong competition in your own family, which you should regard as a unity, how can it be possible to have a peaceful life? This is so contradictory to the spirit of marriage that it is no surprise that it would break up a marriage.

The solution seems to be that if both husband and wife agree to come down from their selfish stance and meet each other midway, then there is a possibility of continuing the relationship. If both partners remain completely stuck in that selfish place, then there is no real solution except for separation.

Certainly though, when both the husband and wife are involved with the practice of Dharma, there are some real solutions possible, even in the case of serious problems. Buddhism teaches that we can go beyond the mistakes we make out of selfishness and arrogance. In particular, the influence of Dharma can teach us that being in a place of competition with your partner — such as feeling jealous of your own husband's or wife's success — is completely useless and destructive. You are one family. By recognizing and feeling that unity, you can give each other complete support and cooperation.

An essential part of practicing the Dharma is that the couple can do meditation in an ongoing way. Meditation develops the qualities of mindfulness and alertness, and it is very helpful to understand exactly what these qualities are and how they work in meditation. As the couple continues along with the practice of meditation, it will have a great calming and clarifying effect on their minds. Within that calmness and clarity will arise understanding and wisdom specific to their own situation. This can help the couple heal their relationship, even if it has been very rocky. Practitioners of Buddhism are certainly not immune to problems in relationship and marriage, but meditation is of great benefit. By virtue of the basic peacefulness of mind that comes from practice, along with an insight into our samsaric condition, the couple learns to cope with the situation and meet each other halfway. The outstanding quality of a good practitioner of Dharma in this regard is that very real progress can be made. It comes about through meditation (including doing retreat practices) and through the guidance and inspiration of a teacher. Again, I am not saying that just by being a Buddhist, all these problems disappear, but there are real possibilities for resolution if you work sincerely and honestly with the teachings and practices of Dharma.

Bardor Tulku Rinpoche

A COMMENTARY ON THE THIRTY-SEVEN PRACTICES OF A BODHISATTVA

As we have seen so far, the Buddhist view of things is that as ordinary beings we are living in a state of confusion, and that until we overcome that confusion there is really no limit to the amount of suffering we can cause for ourselves and others. We saw the importance of renunciation of the psychological and behavioral patterns that perpetuate that confusion, and of the role that spiritual discipline plays on the path. I have discussed monasticism quite a bit, not only because it is of such importance to Buddhism as a whole, but because the basic principles of monasticism are important to all practitioners. In fact, we have seen that the benefits of the practice of the vinaya are available to all practitioners, whether it is on a temporary basis in such practices as the *nyungne* (a two-day intensive practice), or as a lifelong commitment.

Whatever direction we adopt as followers of the Dharma, the development and practice of compassion is absolutely central to our path toward complete enlightenment. In our discussion of relationships, we have seen that while living an ordinary life in the world it is not only possible, but essential, to bring compassion into our basic approach to life, and indeed into everything we do. In fact, the challenges of relationships, work, and community provide exactly the sorts of situations we need to progress.

In Tibetan Buddhism it is traditional to give teachings in conjunction with a particular text. This is how I would like to present a deeper explanation of what it means to live in compassion. The text I will be using is called *The Thirty-Seven Practices of a Bodhisattva*, which was composed by Ngülchu Thogme.

Ngülchu Thogme was a great bodhisattva who lived in Tibet around the 11th century. To say that he was a great bodhisattva means that he went through all of the stages of the bodhisattva path. Having gone through these stages and realized their meaning, he wrote this text as an explanation of that process.

As we go through the teaching, I will also give some explanation of the structure of the text itself. This will be informative about traditional Buddhist scholarship in general, but in particular it will help us make a very focused study of *The Thirty-Seven Practices*. What you will find is that although it is a short text, it is very complete and elegant in its presentation of the principles of mahayana Buddhism.

Like most texts, this has three parts, which can be called in general "the excellence in the beginning, excellence in the middle, and excellence at the end."

The excellence in the beginning is the homage or veneration and the promise to compose the text. The excellence in the middle is the body of the text, which explains the thirty-seven practices. Then the excellence at the end is the conclusion and summary of the text together with the colophon.

The first of these, "the excellence at the beginning," has two parts: the homage and the promise to compose the text. The homage has two parts, which are the brief statement of homage and the explanation of that homage. The brief statement of homage is the initial line of Sanskrit with which the text begins. It says "Namo Lokeshvaraya," which means "Homage to the Lord of the World." Here, "Lokeshvara," which means "Lord of the World," is another name for the Bodhisattva Avalokiteshvara, who is called Chenrezig in Tibetan.

The second part of the homage is the first stanza of the text, which explains the brief Sanskrit line. It says, "I continually pay homage with veneration of body, speech, and mind to the supreme guru and the protector, Avalokiteshvara, who although they see that all things are without coming and going, nevertheless are one-pointedly diligent in accomplishing benefit for beings."

The homage is saying that the supreme guru, which is to say the spiritual friend who teaches the mahayana, and also the Bodhisattva Avalokiteshvara, possess that wisdom that knows the nature of all things. This means they have the wisdom that sees that all things have no true existence and are therefore beyond the eight elaborations or eight conceptually imputed extremes. The eight elaborations include such characteristics as coming and going, permanence and impermanence, being something or being nothing, and so forth. Although they see the nature of all things just as it is, they nevertheless possess a great love and a great compassion that causes them to be tirelessly diligent in accomplishing benefit for beings. In fact, they are so one-pointedly concentrated on this that they only do things that are beneficial for beings. Thogme is saying this about the teacher who teaches one the mahayana, and also the Bodhisattva Arya Avalokiteshvara, who is the compassion of all buddhas, and therefore is the protector of beings who lack a friend, refuge, and protector. He pays homage to them continually with veneration that is physical, verbal, and mental.

The second part of the excellence at the beginning is the promise to compose the text. It is the second stanza of the text and reads, "The sources of all benefit and happiness, the perfect buddhas, come from the practice of genuine Dharma, and that depends upon the knowledge of its implementation. Therefore, I will explain the practice, or implementation of the practice, of the bodhisattvas, who are the children of the Victor."

This stanza is pointing out that all of the temporary benefits and good things that there are in the world, and also the ultimate happiness of liberation and omniscience, all come from the activity of perfect, fully awakened buddhas. However, those buddhas did not begin as buddhas. Instead, their buddhahood came from having properly practiced the Dharma of the mahayana when they were on the path. That path begins with their generation of bodhicitta through the motivation of great compassion. Then it proceeds with the cultivation of all the methods — generosity, morality, patience, diligence, and meditation — along with the aspect of knowledge (prajna) which is the recognition that all things are without any true or inherent existence. Thus through their practice of the path of the six perfections (the first five are concerned with method, and the last one with knowledge), they gathered the two accumulations of merit and wisdom, and in that way they came to attain buddhahood. Their successful gathering of the two accumulations depends only upon their having a proper understanding of how these are to be implemented or practiced. Therefore, those wishing to enter into the path of the mahayana in order to attain buddhahood need to understand the proper practice of these various aspects of bodhisattva training, and that includes both the intention and the conduct, which is the implementation of that intention. Thogme is saying that in this text he will explain the implementation of these things just as they are found in the sutras and commentaries on those sutras of the mahayana. That is his statement of intention or commitment.

The second part is the main body of the text, which consists of thirty-seven stanzas, each of which explains one of the thirty-seven practices of a bodhisattva. This has two sections. The first, which consists of the first seven stanzas, is the preliminaries, or how to enter into the practice of Dharma. The second part, which consists of the remaining thirty stanzas, is the explanation of the actual path, and this is called "the path for the three types of individuals."

The first stanza of the preliminaries is concerned with making the freedom and resources of our human lives meaningful. In the text it says, "At this time at which one has acquired this great ship of freedom and resources, so difficult to acquire, in order to free oneself and others from the ocean of samsara, to cultivate hearing, contemplation, and meditation without distraction throughout day and night is the practice of bodhisattvas."

The meaning of this stanza is that at this time we have acquired a state of tremendous freedom, which is defined as being free from eight unrestful states. The eight unrestful states are being reborn: (1) in the hells; (2) as a preta; (3) as an animal; and (4) as a long-lived god. Even if we are born as a human being, we are born: (5) in a world where no buddha has appeared; (6) as a "barbarian" (which means being born in a place where one has no access to Dharma, even though it might exist in that world); (7) having naturally wrong views toward the Dharma although you have contact with it; and (8) having incomplete faculties such that you cannot comprehend or practice the Dharma. Since we lack those eight kinds of impediments we have what is called freedom or leisure.

In addition to that, we possess ten resources, five of which are called the five intrinsic resources, or personal resources, and five of which are called the five extrinsic or external resources. The five intrinsic resources are: (1) we have been born as human beings; (2) we are born in a central country; (3) we have complete faculties (which means both mentally and with the sense faculties necessary to comprehend and gain access to Dharma); (4) we are not engaged in a counterproductive lifestyle that goes against the Dharma; and (5) we have faith in the Dharma.

The term "central country" can mean one of two things. According to a dharmic description of the world, it is any country to which Dharma has spread; this is the important classification. From a strictly geographical division, "central country" is defined as India, and specifically, Bodhgaya, where the Buddha, having attained the vajra-like samadhi, attained buddhahood. Thus being born in a central country means being born in a place where you have access to

Dharma. In addition to that, we possess the five external resources. These are: (1) that the Buddha appeared in this world; (2) that he taught; (3) that his teachings survive down to the present day; (4) that there are sufficient number of individuals following his teachings so that we can hear about them and gain access to them; and finally, (5) that there are individuals who through great kindness facilitate our entry into the Dharma and our practice of it.

Because we possess these freedoms and resources, we have what is called a precious human existence. This precious human existence is like a great ship in that it is a vehicle we can use to cross the ocean of samsara. However, this precious human body is extremely difficult to acquire. The difficulty of acquiring this precious human body can be explained in three ways: using an analogy, using the idea of the proportion, and through explaining the cause of acquiring it.

The analogy that is found in the *Bodhicaryavatara* is to imagine a blind turtle living in a huge ocean, and that once every hundred years this turtle rises to the surface and sticks its head above the water. Somewhere on the surface of this huge ocean there is also something like a lifesaver, or a yoke. Imagine the probability of that turtle randomly sticking its head, without a particular intention to do so, through that yoke. The probability of this is the same as the probability of our being reborn with a precious human body.

Then there is the explanation with regard to the cause — why it is so difficult to acquire a precious human body. The cause of being born a human being, and especially having a precious human body, is flawless moral discipline. Since the practice of flawless moral discipline is extremely rare, so too is rebirth with a precious human body.

With regard to the proportion, this can be explained in different ways. One way is to say that beings in the hells are as numerous as particles (or you could say grains of dust) in all realms. Sometimes it is explained as particles of dust in a field. In this case, pretas (hungry ghosts) are as common as pieces of chaff in a container used for brewing chang (Tibetan beer). By comparison, human beings are as common as dust motes on top of your fingernail. These examples give the relative proportions. If you want to use personal observation, then you can simply look at the number of insects that you will find in a small area, such as under a single rock, and so on, and compare that with the number of human beings you will find in the same area. In this way, the proportion of beings in those two realms becomes clear. As well, among human beings, most have what is called a "mere human existence," which is to say they do not have all of these eighteen characteristics that were mentioned.

Because this human existence is so difficult to acquire, it is called precious. It is also called precious because it is the basis that we can use to attain liberation and omniscience. In short, we can use this to accomplish either the aim of our own personal liberation or the aim of full awakening for the benefit of others. Understanding this, it is clear that at this time, when we have acquired this rare opportunity, we should not, obviously, waste it. In order to liberate ourselves and others from the ocean of existence, we must make full use of the limited time for which we possess this opportunity. Thus it is the practice of bodhisattvas to listen to the profound instructions of the mahayana, in the presence of a spiritual friend of the mahayana, and to contemplate and analyze the meaning of what they have heard through the four great reasonings and so forth, throughout day and night, in all situations, without the slightest distraction. Then having properly understood them, it is the practice of bodhisattvas to meditate upon these instructions, by means of which they make this freedom and these resources of the precious human life meaningful.

The second stanza is concerned with relinquishing our birthplace or homeland. The reason for this is that the birthplace is described here as the source of the three poisons. In the text it says, "In that place, one's attachment for friends and family pulses like a river, one's aversion for enemies blazes like fire. One possesses the thick, dark obscurity of that bewilderment and apathy that forgets what is to be undertaken and what is to be avoided. Therefore it is the practice of bodhisattvas to abandon their homeland."

This explanation needs to be accompanied by the statement that what is described here is the kind of radical renunciation that a perfect practitioner needs to practice. This is not saying that all practitioners need to, or can, do this. It is however the type of radical renunciation that is necessary for someone who wishes to practice in the most complete manner. When a bodhisattva has acquired this supremely valuable — and impermanent — opportunity of a precious human birth, in order to make the fullest use of it, they are going to consciously choose the environment in which they live. The reason a bodhisattva will leave his or her homeland is that when one is attempting to practice Dharma, if one remains in one's homeland, then due to attachment to family and friends — attachment here means both the emotional attachment itself and all of the subsidiary attachments that leads to, such as the need to promote the interests of the family, to support the family, and so on — the bodhisattva risks becoming more and more involved in endless existence in the creation of further karma. As well, because they are attached to some people, they will naturally have aversion for those who threaten the interests of those people. Thus there will be dislike and aversion for certain people in one's homeland. That kind of aversion is like a fire that burns up our virtue, and the attachment is like rapids in a river, disturbing the mind. Because of these two things, there will be an obscuration of one's judgment as to which actions are to be undertaken and which are to be avoided. Thus there will be an impairment of mindfulness and alertness and therefore an increase of bewilderment, like a thick and obscuring fog. In short, it is the practice of bodhisattvas to abandon their homeland because it is the root of attachment and aversion and is therefore the source of numerous defects.

The third stanza follows from that, and is concerned with the virtues of relying upon solitude or isolation, because solitude is the source of qualities. It says, "Through abandoning negative environments, one's mental afflictions gradually diminish. Through being undistracted, one's virtuous endeavors naturally flourish. Because one's awareness is lucid, certainty about Dharma is born. It is therefore the practice of bodhisattvas to rely upon solitude."

When bodhisattvas have abandoned their homeland, they then need to rely upon solitude. Having abandoned a negative or harmful environment, they need to consciously choose an environment conducive to practice. The reason is that through relying upon solitude, all the various mental afflictions — attachment, aversion, and so forth — will become weaker over time through lack of stimulation. Therefore the bodhisattva's moral discipline will remain pure. Because they are without the need for involvement in a lot of troublesome things to sustain and protect their family, such as business endeavors and so on, because they are without distraction and occupations, their mind will remain one-pointedly in samadhi and they will have the time and space to be diligent in the cultivation of samadhi. In short, all their virtuous practices of body, speech, and mind will naturally increase. Because of this diligent application of meditation practice, their mind will come to rest in a state of tranquility, their intelligence will become more flexible and clear. Their awareness being more lucid, through their examination they will have a clearer understanding of the meaning of the genuine Dharma, generating a greater certainty about that meaning. Because of this certainty, all aspects of their training — moral discipline, meditative stability, and knowledge of the nature of things — will flourish. Therefore it is the practice of bodhisattvas to rely upon isolation or solitude, which is an environment conducive to practice.

The fourth stanza deals with abandoning obsessive concern with the things of this life, specifically through the recollection of impermanence. The text reads, "One will be sepa-

61

rated from those companions, friends, and family whom one has accompanied for a long time. One will leave behind all the wealth and possessions that have been acquired with such exertion. The traveler of one's consciousness will leave the guesthouse of this body. It is therefore the practice of bodhisattvas to let go of this life."

The meaning of this is that no matter how long you are with someone in this life, eventually anyone you accompany will be separated from you. This applies even to immediate family members such as your parents. They are your parents for your whole life, but either they will die first, or you will die first. In either case, separation is certain. No matter how many friends and how much family you have, at the time of death separation is final. All of the wealth and possessions you have accumulated through tremendous exertion, as well as all of the things you have accomplished through great suffering and at the risk of the accumulation of tremendous negative karma, will be completely left behind when you die. They will not do you an atom's worth of good at that point.

It is certain that you will leave everything behind at death, and you will have no power whatsoever to take anything with you. Not only will you leave behind all the people and things to which you are attached, but this thing to which you are most attached, your body — this aggregate of flesh and blood and bone — will be left completely behind by your consciousness. It is as though your consciousness were a traveler and your body were a hotel that the traveler remained in for one night. Just as the traveler moves on and leaves the hotel behind without a thought, in the same way, when your consciousness is separated from your body at death, the connection between the two will be severed forever. In short, when you die you will go on alone. Thus all of the things that seem so important in the limited context of this life, all the troublesome things of this life that cause us to accumulate so much negative karma — such as attempting to conquer or subdue your enemies, attempting to help your friends, and so on — all these activities will be of no use to you when you die. Therefore, through the recollection of death and impermanence, relinquishing concern with these things is the practice of bodhisattvas.

The fifth stanza is concerned with abandoning negative companions who cause conditions that are adverse to practice. It says in the text, "Those whose company causes one's three poisons to flourish, therefore causing the impairment of the activities of hearing, contemplating, and meditating, who bring about the ruin of love and compassion—it is the practice of bodhisattvas to abandon negative companions." Now the meaning of this is that there are those whose company causes our mental afflictions to naturally increase and therefore our positive qualities, such as love and compassion, to naturally decrease. Such friends or companions cut off the life (literally, the "aorta") of liberation. Their company causes our three poisons to increase; therefore it prevents us from engaging in those activities that are the principal causes of attaining liberation. Therefore all of our virtues in general, and especially the specific root mahayana virtues of love and compassion and bodhicitta—in short, whatever virtues we possessed up to that point—will decrease and we will not acquire any new ones. Such companions also include spiritual teachers who lead people on an incorrect path, as well as friends who have a negative influence. Viewing them like vicious predatory animals, it is the practice of bodhisattvas to abandon their company.

The sixth stanza is the converse of the fifth, since it is concerned with reliance upon spiritual friends who create conditions conducive to practice and development. It says, "Holy spiritual friends, reliance upon whom causes all of one's defects to be exhausted and all of one's qualities to flourish like the waxing moon—it is the practice of bodhisattvas to treasure such friends even more than their own bodies."

This stanza points out that, just as there are those who are negative influences upon us, there are also those who are tremendous positive influences. Positive influences are defined as persons with whom any connection causes our virtue to flourish and our defects to diminish. Such people influence us in such a way that whatever defects we have — attachment, aversion, and so on — naturally start to diminish. We become more involved with hearing, contemplation, and meditation. As well, all of our qualities — love, compassion, bodhicitta, and so on — naturally seem to flourish like the waxing moon. Such influences, which may be spiritual friends who lead us on a correct path, and also friends in general who are a good influence, are to be relied upon. Not only are they to be relied upon, but it is the practice of bodhisattvas to treasure such friends who are good influences even more than they treasure their own bodies because these friends bring such benefit.

The final stanza of this initial set of seven stanzas concerned with the preliminaries is about going for refuge. This means how to enter into the teachings and the path. It says, "How could mundane gods, who are themselves fettered in the prison of samsara, be able to protect us? It is therefore the practice of bodhisattvas to go for refuge to the Three Jewels which are infallible sources of refuge."

The purpose, in general, of seeking the protection of a source of refuge is to obtain liberation from samsara, and not merely to accomplish temporary prosperity in this life. In particular, from the point of view of a practitioner of the mahayana (a bodhisattva), the purpose is to be able to liberate all beings. Therefore we must take refuge in those who themselves are actually liberated from samsara. In the mahayana context, we go for refuge not merely for this life, but until we have attained perfect buddhahood, and we do so not only for our own benefit but because it is our aim to bring about the liberation of all beings. Therefore we go for refuge in order to be able to begin that process and achieve that end.

For that reason, we cannot seek refuge from beings who themselves are bound in samsara. This refers to mundane beings, such as various gods, spirits, nagas, gods of trees and forests and mountains and rivers, gods of the elements, and so on. No matter how powerful they may be, they cannot cause us to achieve even a higher rebirth or liberation — let alone buddhahood. They cannot protect us from the lower realms or from the sufferings of samsara. They cannot do any of this because they are still fettered in the prison of karma, mental afflictions, and the result of such patterns — which is the experience of samsara — without any control over this themselves. Since they cannot save themselves from lower rebirth and cannot cause themselves a higher rebirth, how could they be expected to afford that kind of refuge to someone else? Therefore, it is the practice of bodhisattvas not to go for refuge to mundane spirits but to go for refuge to that extraordinary source which will never fail us and can actually protect us from the dangers of existence (i.e., rebirth in the realms of samsara) and tranquility (i.e., the partial nirvana of an arhat), that is to say, the Three Jewels — the Buddha, Dharma, and Sangha. Thus it is the practice of bodhisattvas to go for refuge to the Three Jewels with an attitude of utterly entrusting themselves to those sources of refuge.

QUESTIONS AND ANSWERS

Question: I'm a little unclear as to how to understand, in this context, the abandoning of attachment to family, work, and so forth. This seems quite difficult in today's world.

Rinpoche: That's quite a common question. To be frank, people in Western countries have an easier time with the issue of attachment and renunciation than Asians do. That is especially true about the part of the text that says that it is the practice of bodhisattvas to abandon their homeland. That is a much more common thing in the West than in Asia. In Asia, people have lived in the same place for generation after generation after generation, and they have no intention of ever leaving it. It is much more difficult for them. In the West, you live in one state or town for two or three years, then you leave and live somewhere else. Also with regard

65

to attachment to family, it is evident from my experience living in the West that people are far less attached to their parents, in particular, than Asians.

The bigger issue here is that all these explanations of the practices of bodhisattvas are just that, they are practices of *bodhisattvas*. We are, at this point, followers of buddhas and bodhisattvas; we are not really bodhisattvas. Thus at this point, we are cultivating aspiration bodhicitta, and our cultivation of the implementation of that—implementation bodhicitta—has to be very gradual. Therefore you do what you can of this.

Question: How can I get my family to understand and accept my practice of Dharma? I know it will help them, ultimately speaking.

Rinpoche: That is also a very common situation. I think that as long as you are not doing anything that is harmful to your parents, to your family, your spouse or partner, then you have the right to do what you want. The practice of Dharma, as you say, will ultimately help them. Thus it is best if they understand that what you are doing is good for yourself and good for them. If they do not understand, simply continue to practice as much as you can and make aspirations and dedication of merit for their benefit.

This is another area where there is a distinction to be made between Asia and the West. In Asia, family unity is stressed, so it is very difficult to do something that your parents are against. It seems that in the West there is much more emphasis on independence, so you should use that independence positively.

Question: Could you give some general advice about developing faith in the Dharma?

Rinpoche: Basically you can do that by studying the sorts of materials that help you develop faith and certainty. It is especially recommended to read the biographies of great teachers of the past, because their examples are very inspiring. However, something needs to be said about how to relate to them. When you read the biography of someone like Jetsun Milarepa, for example, the attitude that you should develop, the effect the biography *should* have on you, is thinking that if even a great being like Jetsun Milarepa had to engage in such tremendous austerities, then how much more necessary must it be for an ordinary individual like ourselves to practice with great diligence. In that way, you feel encouraged to practice. The reason I mention this is that sometimes when people read such stories they are actually intimidated by them. They think, "If such a great being as Jetsun Milarepa had so much difficulty on the path, then there is no hope whatsoever for a lowly individual such as myself. Therefore, I might as well just give up right now!" These biographies do not exist in order to discourage you or make you feel inadequate. They exist in order to give you an understanding of how much diligence and persistence is necessary. Thus reading biographies is very helpful.

As well, reading about Dharma in general is highly recommended, especially those aspects which you can relate to and which inspire you. Sometimes study itself produces faith, but specifically, increasing your understanding of Dharma increases your confidence in its validity. Through understanding what it means, you come more and more to understand that it is valid and true. That is really the source of faith.

When you are reading biographies, you need to understand them in context. For example, there are many versions of the previous lives of the Buddha, one of which is called "The One Thousand Births," another which is called "One Hundred Births," and so on. He is said to have had, immediately preceding his life as the Buddha, five hundred pure births and five hundred impure births. Throughout all of these, the Buddha, as a bodhisattva, did many extraordinary things in order to increase his realization. People are put off by some of this. For example, in many lifetimes, he actually gave up his life—gave up his body—in order to benefit another being. This can discourage people. They think that if even the Buddha had to do this extremely difficult thing so many times then they might as well give up. You have to place it in context, however. The context here is the point at which someone is on the path. Although as ordinary beings we would find it impossible to do some of those things now, we would not find it impossible to give someone a plate of food, or to give someone a needle and thread. These would be normal and natural acts of generosity for us. When someone has attained the realization of a bodhisattva, giving away all of his or her possessions, food, or even their very body is as natural and effortless as giving away a plate of food is for us. However, we do not perform these extraordinary actions until they become possible and appropriate. If you understand that point, you will not find these stories discouraging. Because bodhisattvas *can* do those things, then it is appropriate and beneficial for them to do them.

(END OF QUESTIONS AND ANSWERS)

Thus far we have gone through the first seven stanzas, which are on the preliminaries for entering the path. Next we will begin the thirty remaining stanzas which are concerned with the actual implementation of the path. As you will remember from the brief outline I gave at the beginning, the path is divided into three stages, which correspond to the three types of individuals.

In keeping with this, the next stanza is an explanation of the path for the lesser individual. "Lesser individual" is defined here as someone who abandons wrongdoing because he or she is afraid of the sufferings of the lower realms. Thus a lesser individual is someone who is attempting to accomplish a higher rebirth, not liberation. In the text it says, "The intolerable sufferings of the lower states were taught by Buddha Shakyamuni to be the result of actions that are wrongdoing. Therefore, it is the practice of bodhisattvas to abstain from wrongdoing even at the cost of their lives."

Here the text is saying that merely hearing of the sufferings of the three lower states causes terror to arise because these sufferings are so horrendous. Therefore, if and when someone actually has to experience them, it goes without saying that they are intolerably painful. However, these sufferings do not "just happen." They do not arise without any cause whatsoever. As well, they are not produced by an "inappropriate cause." This means a cause that could not really be their cause, such as the actions of an external creator or something like that. In other words, they are not an imposition from outside. The suffering comes as a result of previous wrongdoings by the same being who comes to experience that suffering. "Wrongdoing" refers to such actions as the ten forms of non-virtuous action — three of body, four of speech, three of mind, and so forth. Since the Buddha knew that all these sufferings are the result of wrongdoing, this was what he taught. Because bodhisattvas understand this, because they understand that suffering is the result of wrongdoing, then even at the cost of their lives they will never engage in wrongdoing. Thus it is the practice of bodhisattvas to very carefully choose actions and to distinguish between what should be undertaken and what should be avoided. This is called the path of the lesser individual because it is the first part of the path; it is the foundation of the rest of the path.

The next stanza, the second, deals with the path of an intermediate individual. An "intermediate individual" is someone who not only wishes to escape the sufferings of the lower realms, but also recognizes that all of samsara is a state of suffering and therefore, without being attached to the pleasures of existence, wishes to obtain liberation. The text says, "The pleasures of the three realms (or three types of existence) are like dew on the bladetips of grass. They will be destroyed in an instant. Therefore, it is the practice of bodhisattvas to undertake the attainment of that supreme state of unchanging liberation."

This means that whatever pleasures there are in the three realms of samsara (the realm of desire, the realm of form, and the formless realm) or in the three levels of existence (existence below the earth, on the earth, and above the earth)—in short, anywhere in samsara, all these defiled states of happiness or pleasure are impermanent. They are as certain to end as a drop of dew that appears on the tip of a blade of grass before dawn is certain to evaporate. Because these things are so ephemeral, they are unfit to be objects of attachment. What is fit to be undertaken, on the other hand, is a state of happiness that is stable, permanent, and unchanging. This means the state of perfect liberation from samsara. Therefore, it is the practice of bodhisattvas to generate the intention to attain such liberation, through the inspiration of an extraordinary renunciation that recognizes that only liberation is a worthy goal.

As was mentioned, this stanza refers to the aspiration of the intermediate individual. This is so because he or she is more advanced than someone who merely wishes to obtain a better rebirth within samsara, but is less advanced than someone who aspires to the full enlightenment of a buddha. The path of individual liberation from samsara, if pursued to its conclusion, results in the attainment of the state of an arhat. Those who are pursuing this goal may see it as the ultimate state of enlightenment, but it is not. Someone who has obtained arhatship remains in a profound meditative state that is free from suffering for an inconceivably long period of time. Then fully enlightened buddhas communicate with them and guide them onto the path of compassionate activity that finally leads them to full buddhahood. From a mahayana point of view, the pursuit of arhatship is considered a serious delay and sidetrack. Thus, while bodhisattvas aspire to liberation from samsara, they do so in the context of the greater goal of buddhahood.

This greater goal is the subject of the remaining twenty-eight stanzas in this section on the main part of the path, and that is why it is called an explanation of the path of the "greater individual." Such an individual is defined as someone who wishes to transcend not only samsara, but also even the temporary or imperfect nirvana of an arhat. Thus the path of the greater individual is the endeavor to attain that supreme buddhahood that is beyond the extremes of existence and peace through a path that is an integration of compassion and the realization of emptiness.

The explanation of this path has three parts. The first is the generation of bodhicitta — the intention to attain supreme awakening — as the intention of the path. The second is the meditation on the two bodhicittas, relative and absolute, as the actual implementation of that intention. Then the third is the training in the observances connected with those two bodhicittas.

The first, the initial generation of bodhicitta, is as follows: "Our mothers are beings who throughout beginningless time have been kind to us, and if these beings are suffering, what good is our own happiness? It is therefore the practice of bodhisattvas to generate bodhicitta in order to liberate innumerable sentient beings."

What distinguishes the path of the greater individual from the first two is the recognition that just as we are suffering, so are all beings. Knowing that, the greater individual finds the idea of abandoning all beings and simply attaining individual liberation to be inappropriate and intolerable. This is because throughout beginningless existence, all of the various beings that there are have at many times been extremely kind to us. They have in fact, under various circumstances, loved us more than their own lives, and have given up their own lives and welfare for us. Thus all of these beings of the six states of samsara have been our mother at one time or another. Right now, they are undergoing the sufferings of samsara in general. Especially, most of them are in the lower states and are undergoing horrific sufferings that last for a very long time and will never come to an end, in and of themselves.

71

What good would it be if, knowing that, we were to ignore that fact and simply undertake our own happiness and liberation, as is the case of the lesser individual who undertakes merely to secure temporary happiness through a higher rebirth, or as is the case with the intermediate individual, who undertakes personal liberation through attainment of the state of an arhat? We would have abandoned all beings; they would still be suffering. In fact, to undertake such a personal liberation, such personal happiness and welfare, and to ignore the welfare of other beings would be extremely shameful and unfair. This is considered by those who are described here as "greater individuals" to be a horrific mistake. Therefore, in order to be able to liberate all beings without exception from samsara, it is the practice of bodhisattvas to generate bodhicitta, preceded by the cultivation of love and compassion, just as it has been generated by all the buddhas and bodhisattvas of the past.

The second part of the path of a greater individual is the application of that intention by cultivation of the two bodhicittas. This has two parts: the first is the cultivation of relative bodhicitta, and the second is the cultivation of absolute bodhicitta.

The first of these, the cultivation of relative bodhicitta, has two parts. The first of these is, in even placement (which means in meditation) to exchange oneself for others. The second part is known as taking adverse conditions onto the path in post-meditation. (Post-meditation means whenever we are not meditating.)

The first of these, the even placement or meditation practice of relative bodhicitta, is explained in the next stanza, which is the eleventh of the thirty-seven stanzas of the central section of the text. It says, "All sufferings without exception come from desiring one's own happiness. Perfect buddhahood comes from altruism. Therefore, it is the practice of bodhisattvas to completely exchange their own happiness for the sufferings of others."

This means that whatever sufferings there are in samsara, large and small, all without exception come from cherishing and desiring our own happiness at the expense of others. The ultimate bliss of buddhahood, along with whatever goodness there is in the world and beyond this world — in short, all happiness whatsoever — comes from desiring the happiness of others. In other words, happiness comes from altruism. Therefore, cherishing others more than ourselves, being willing to give all of our happiness and virtue to others, letting go of concern with our own welfare, being willing to take on ourselves all of the wrongdoing and sufferings of others, is the practice of bodhisattvas. That is the meditation practice of relative bodhicitta.

The next section in the text is the post-meditation practice of relative bodhicitta, which is how to take adverse conditions onto the path. This has four sections. The first is how to take the four undesirables onto the path; the second is how to take the two intolerables onto the path; the third is how to take prosperity and ruin onto the path; and the fourth is how to take attachment and aversion onto the path.

The first of these, how to take the four undesirables onto the path, has four parts. These are: (1) how to take loss onto the path; (2) how to take suffering onto the path; (3) how to take calumny onto the path; and (4) how to take verbal abuse onto the path.

The first of these, loss, means financial loss or loss of possessions. This is explained in the twelfth stanza. It says, "When someone through great desire steals or causes another to steal one's own possessions or wealth, it is the practice of bodhisattvas to dedicate their bodies, possessions, and virtues of past, present, and future to that person."

The meaning of this is that when a being out of great desire to possess those things takes your wealth, possessions, and so on, or gets someone else to steal these for them, a bodhisattva does not respond with anger and attempt to seek vengeance. In fact, they become even more concerned with benefiting that being. They become willing to give even their bodies, their possessions, and even all the virtues they have accumulated in the past, are accumulating in the present, and will accumulate in the future. In short, in response to theft, it is the practice of bodhisattvas to dedicate everything they have to that thief. That is how bodhisattvas take the loss of possessions onto the path.

The next stanza, the thirteenth, deals with how to take suffering onto the path. Here, this refers to suffering born of someone else's abuse, specifically extreme physical abuse. The text says, "When, without oneself having done anything wrong whatsoever, someone else goes so far as to cut off one's head, to take that person's wrongdoing into oneself through the power of compassion is the practice of a bodhisattva."

The situation described here is an extreme one, to show how far bodhisattvas will go. In this situation, the bodhisattva has done nothing whatsoever to the aggressor that justifies their abuse. Nevertheless, that person not only mutilates him or her by cutting off their arms and legs and so on, but cuts off the best of their limbs, the head. Even though they are killing you, a bodhisattva would not respond in turn by kicking or striking them, but would be concerned with the wrongdoing and negative karma that person was accumulating, because they know that killing will cause the other to be reborn in hell. And when they get out of the hell realms, they will have a short life, and a liking for killing, so they will kill again, and the cycle will continue over and over. A bodhisattva would not be thinking about his or her personal suffering, but about how much suffering the murderer was accruing through perpetrating violence. Therefore, through great compassion, a bodhisattva would wish to experience this suffering in their stead, and would attempt to take that person's wrongdoing onto themselves. That is how bodhisattvas take the suffering of physical abuse onto the path.

The fourteenth stanza deals with the third part of this section, taking slander onto the path: "When someone proclaims various unpleasant things about you, to the point where they fill the galaxy with rumor, it is the practice of a bodhisattva, with a loving mind, to only proclaim the other person's good qualities."

In this case, someone is saying terrible things about you behind your back. By being extremely vigorous in doing so, they manage to fill the galaxy with unpleasant and untrue rumors about you. No matter how widespread these rumors are, a bodhisattva would not attempt to seek vengeance by spreading nasty rumors in return. Beyond that, the bodhisattva would want to make that person happy. They must be really unhappy to be spreading slander, and so in order to make them happy, a bodhisattva would diligently try to talk about that person's good points, and fill the galaxy with that. This is how bodhisattvas bring slander or calumny onto the path.

The fourth and final part of this section is how to bring verbal abuse on the path. The fifteenth stanza says, "When, in the midst of an assembly of many beings, someone proclaims one's hidden defects with unpleasant words, it is the practice of a bodhisattva to respectfully pay homage to that person, with the perception that they are a spiritual friend."

This describes a situation where there is a gathering of many people. In the midst of that, someone starts to tell you terrible things about yourself, cataloging your mundane and dharmic defects. They are actually trying to find and reveal your hidden defects, things that might not be obvious to the other people in the gathering, using various unpleasant forms of language and expressions. A bodhisattva would not only refrain from anger and responding in kind, but, instead of focusing on the negative motivation of the abuser, would think about the value of what they were learning about themselves from what the person said. Therefore, they would treat the abuser with the respect accorded a teacher, because this person had shown them something about themselves. That is how bodhisattvas bring verbal abuse onto the path.

Next comes the second set of adverse conditions, which is taking the "two intolerables" onto the path. This has two parts: the first is taking betrayal onto the path, and the second is taking denigration onto the path.

Taking betrayal onto the path is explained in the sixteenth stanza: "When someone whom one has cherished as one's own child views one as an enemy, it is the practice of a bodhisattva to love them even more, as a mother would love a child who has become ill."

This describes a situation where someone who you have only benefited, someone for whom you have cared as if they were your own child, views you as an enemy and with body, speech, and mind tries to harm you as much as they can. The relationship could be one of Dharmic connection. In the most extreme instance, the betrayal is from someone to whom you have given empowerment, transmission, and instruction. It could also be a relationship in which you had given material support and care. A bodhisattva would not only not be angry and try to get revenge, but instead he or she would take the attitude of a mother whose child becomes mentally ill. If a child becomes mentally ill and even starts to physically attack the parents, the parents do not become angry and try to harm the child. They will be more concerned about the child's welfare because they see that the child is seriously ill. A bodhisattva relates to anyone who betrays or abuses him or her in the same way. A mother in that situation would think, "When will my child be well again; what do I need to do to help them become well?" In the same way a bodhisattva thinks, "This person who is harming me has come under the power of mental afflictions. Why can't they be free of mental afflictions? What do I have to do to free them from mental afflictions?" Thinking this way, a bodhisattva would be even more concerned and more loving towards this person. That is how bodhisattvas take betrayal onto the path.

The second intolerable is denigration, which means here what we would call snubbing. "When, through the power of arrogance, someone who is one's social equal or inferior snubs one, it is the practice of a bodhisattva to put them on top of one's head with the same respect as if they were one's guru."

This refers to a situation involving someone who, according to the criteria of your society, is your equal or inferior in a professional or social situation. Despite being an equal, because they are arrogant or proud, they revile you, snub you, and denigrate you in various ways. In such a situation, a bodhisattva does not respond by getting into a competition of arrogance to see who can "out snub" the other. Instead, a bodhisattva responds with even more respect and courtesy to that person, as though they were even one's own guru. That is how bodhisattvas take denigration onto the path.

The third aspect of taking difficulties onto the path connected with relative bodhicitta is taking prosperity and disaster onto the path. This has two parts, the first of which is taking disaster onto the path.

That is explained in the eighteenth stanza, which says, "When you are impoverished, without even what you need to survive, and continually reviled by people, struck by strong illness and harmed by demons, it is the practice of a bodhisattva to take, in addition, all the suffering and wrongdoing of beings onto themselves, without any hesitation or fear."

This refers to a situation where everything is going wrong. You are either impoverished from the very start or as a result of theft or loss. In short you are so poor that you do not even have enough food to keep yourself healthy and enough clothing to keep yourself warm. In addition to that, you are continually denigrated and berated by other people. Then you are struck by serious illness, such as leprosy, and also are harmed by different kinds of spirits from all directions, from above, below, and all around you. When everything possible is going wrong, and you have intense suffering, a bodhisattva would not think of his or her own misery. Instead, extrapolating from their own experience of suffering, the bodhisattva would deduce from that the suffering of all beings. They would think, "If I find this so hard to bear, how much worse must it be for all of these beings, many of whom have even worse sufferings." That would cause the bodhisattva to generate tremendous compassion, and thus to aspire that their own personal suffering serve in the place of the sufferings of all other beings, and that they alone would have to suffer these intolerable things. A bodhisattva in that situation would not only accept his or her own disaster but, without hesitation, wish that the disasters of all other beings be included within theirs, and that all other beings be free of suffering.

The next stanza, the nineteenth, explains how bodhisattvas bring prosperity onto the path: "When one is famous and beings bow to one, when one is as wealthy as Vaisravana, it is the practice of a bodhisattva, seeing the prosperity of existence as meaningless, to be without vanity."

This refers to the opposite situation, where a bodhisattva finds him or herself incredibly affluent and prosperous, in a high social position, and renowned — perhaps even world-famous — and thus respected and bowed to by all manner of beings. Having even the wealth of the king Vaisravana, who is said to be the wealthiest of the gods, a bodhisattva would not be arrogant, knowing all the time that these mundane attainments or prosperity are as ephemeral as the dew on blades of grass. Seeing such wealth as transitory and unstable as a flash of lightning, as insubstantial as a water bubble, he or she would see these attainments as valueless, like the discarded skin of a snake. Thus the bodhisattva would have no vanity or arrogance based upon their social position, wealth, and so forth. That is how bodhisattvas take prosperity onto the path.

The fourth part of taking relative bodhicitta onto the path is concerned with attachment and aversion. This has two parts, the first of which is taking aversion onto the path. That is described in the twentieth stanza, which says, "If one does not subdue one's own enemy which is one's own aggression, then as much as one subdues external enemies they will only increase. Therefore, it is the practice of bodhisattvas to tame their own minds with the 'armed forces' of love and compassion."

The most difficult enemy to tame is the real enemy, our own mental afflictions, and in particular the aggression which is within our own mind. If we tame the internal or true enemy, which is our own aggression, then just as smoke will no longer arise from an extinguished fire, all of our external enemies and spirits will be pacified effortlessly. On the other hand, if we do not subdue our own aggression, then no matter how many external enemies we succeed in conquering, there will only be more. They will be inexhaustible. Therefore, it is the practice of bodhisattvas to subdue the internal enemy of our own aggression with the force of love, which is the desire that our external enemies be happy, and compassion, which is the desire that our external enemies be free from suffering. Through the application of these, the "armed forces" of love and compassion, bodhisattvas weaken and finally eradicate the internal mental afflictions. That is how aversion is taken onto the path.

The next stanza, the twenty-first, deals with taking attachment onto the path: "Desirable things are like salt water. As much as you enjoy them, they increase your craving. Therefore, it is the practice of bodhisattvas to immediately abandon whatever things generate attachment within them."

Pleasant experiences — enjoyable sights, sounds, tastes, smells, and tactile sensations — all of these things, no matter how much we get of them, are never enough. This is because the process of enjoying them creates more desire for them. The enjoyments of the senses are really like drinking salt water, which instead of quenching thirst actually increases it. Through recognizing that attachment to external pleasures is a source of disaster in this and future lives, it is the practice of bodhisattvas to abandon anything that causes them attachment, and especially to be content with the bare minimum needed to survive. That is how bodhisattvas take attachment onto the path, according to relative bodhicitta.

The next section of the text deals with the cultivation of absolute bodhicitta. This has two parts. The first is meditating without fixation on the nature of mind that is without elaboration in even-placement meditation. The second is abandoning the false imputation of reality or truth to objects of experience that inspire attachment or aversion.

The first of these parts of the meditation on absolute bodhicitta is as follows: "All of these things that appear are not other than one's mind. And that mind itself has from the very beginning been beyond elaboration. Knowing this, it is the practice of bodhisattvas not to generate the imputation of true existence to apprehended objects and an apprehending cognition or subject."

Whatever things appear to us — the external environment and its contents, i.e., all the things we experience as objects of experience — do not possess the characteristics imputed to them. The characteristics of things are merely your own mental imputations and do not exist in these things from their own side. Therefore, what we experience is empty of the characteristics that we impute on the basis of experience. Since the imputations are made by your mind, those characteristics, those imputed characteristics which you think you are experiencing externally, are not other than your own mind.

As well, the mind itself, that which makes these imputations, has from the very beginning been beyond all elaboration. This is to say that from the very beginning it has been neither something nor nothing. It is not permanent and it is not impermanent, and so on. There is nothing that can be said about it, truly, that actually defines it. Therefore all the *objects of experience*, and *that which experiences those objects* (or that for which those objects arise in experience) are of the same fundamental nature. Recognizing that nature to be what it is, bodhisattvas no longer generate the concept in their mind of truly existent external objects (i.e., having an inherent existence separate from the experience of them), or of a truly existent mind or cognition that has an existence separate from experience. Thus bodhisattvas do not generate in their minds any conceptual imputation of the inherent or true existence of perceived characteristics. In that way, they meditate upon emptiness beyond elaboration.

The next section is the post-meditation practice of bodhicitta. That has two parts. The first is how to relinquish fixation on objects of experience that inspire attachment. The second is how to relinquish fixation on the imputed reality of objects of experience that inspire aversion.

The twenty-third stanza is concerned with the first of these. It says, "When you encounter a pleasant object, it is to be viewed as appearing as beautiful or pleasant but without true reality, like the appearance of a rainbow in summer. In that way, it is the practice of bodhisattvas to relinquish craving and attachment."

This stanza deals with situations where you encounter something pleasant, such as friends, relatives, or other persons to whom you are attached, or a sensory experience that you conceive of as pleasant — beautiful forms, pleasant sounds, and so on — or the internal experience of pleasure and comfort. Bodhisattvas view it as having no more substantial or true existence than the appearance of a rainbow in summer. The appearance of a rainbow, which is a vivid and distinct appearance from the perspective of the viewer, nevertheless has no solidity and does not exist as what it appears to be. In the same way, the bodhisattva understands that pleasant objects, while they may appear in that way, nevertheless have no inherent or innate quality that makes them what they appear to be. Viewing pleasant appearances as being without true reality, we do not generate concepts such as "this is my friend," "this is beautiful," "this is pleasant," and so on. Realizing that such concepts are merely our imputation, and no longer taking that object to have those characteristics in and of itself, is the practice of bodhisattvas for stopping fixation on, and craving for, pleasant objects.

The second section of the post-meditation practice of absolute bodhicitta concerns how to relinquish fixation on the reality of objects that inspire aversion. This is the twenty-fourth stanza, which says: "The experience of various sufferings is like the death of one's child in a dream. We suffer from taking deluded projections, deluded appearances, to be real. It is therefore the practice of bodhisattvas, when they encounter adverse conditions, to view them as bewilderment."

This verse deals with the experience of encountering something unpleasant, such as an enemy or a demon, or unpleasant forms, sounds, smells, etc., or the mental experience of suffering. In the example of dreaming that one's child has died — when in fact the child doesn't really exist and therefore cannot and does not die — within the limited context of the dream you do suffer and grieve over the child's death until you awaken from the dream. Likewise, bodhisattvas regard unpleasant appearances as projections produced by their own bewilderment, and recognize that it is only through mistaking these projections to be real that these things actually cause suffering (through thinking "this is my enemy," "this is unpleasant," and so forth). To not generate those concepts or imputations and to see that these are mere projections and do not exist from their own side — that is the practice of bodhisattvas for taking objects that inspire aversion onto the path.

QUESTIONS AND ANSWERS

Question: Could you explain some more about the attitude of exchanging ourselves for others? How would we experience that, or see it, or know that it is happening, depending on where we are on the path?

Rinpoche: When you are doing the practice of exchanging yourself for others and of taking the sufferings of others into yourself, at a certain point you might start to have the conviction that you have actually managed to exchange them, that you have actually managed to take the sufferings of others into yourself and to give them your happiness. Through having that conviction you might actually become ill or something. When that happens, that is not actually exchanging yourself for others. It is a symptom of a very strong fixation on self, because you *cannot* exchange yourself for others. The whole idea of exchanging yourself for others is simply a method of training the mind. We use this method because our entire problem is this whole idea of "I." It is always, "I need to be happy," "I need to not be suffering," "I am the most important being in the universe." Since that is the cause of our suffering, then in order to destroy that, we take the opposite stance. We try and reverse that by exchanging concern for ourselves with concern for others. Essentially, though, this is being done to train the mind. Initially it mostly benefits the practitioner, by lessening fixation on a self.

Because this is lessening the fixation, if the person has especially strong fixation on the self, and therefore has great fear about actually succeeding in this exchange, then they might experience some kind of illness and so on. The illness is not coming from somebody else, however. It is not that you are actually taking other people's negative karma into you. You do not, as an ordinary person, have the power to do that. Bodhisattvas do have the power to do that. They can actu-

83

ally take things, in a certain way, out of beings. But when an ordinary practitioner experiences it, it is something else.

Question: It seems to me that it would be a bit arrogant to simply disregard the sufferings we encounter as delusional. Could you comment on that?

Rinpoche: It is not actually arrogance to see it that way because, for one thing, it is accurate. Suffering is not a thing in itself. It is an interplay. If it is recognized as not having true existence from its own side, that in itself removes one of the elements that allows suffering to occur. When you recognize that you are suffering because you identify something as "suffering," then by recognizing it as a projection it actually pacifies the suffering. In other words, recognizing that you are suffering because you think you are suffering helps overcome the suffering.

Therefore this viewpoint is not a denial of suffering. It is recognition of the actual status of the experience that we call suffering. The approach of attempting to pacify suffering by really plumbing the depths of how miserable you are does not work. For example, if you have a fire and you want the fire to go out, if you add wood to the fire you are not going to smother it. It will only feed it. If you somehow managed to pull all the fuel out of the fire, the fire will go out because the fire depends on the fuel. It works the same way when you remove the concept of reality that you impute on the basis of what you experience as suffering. Because the suffering *depends on* that concept of reality, the suffering is pacified. If on the other hand, you think, "This is suffering; this is real," you are maintaining the conditions for it to continue.

Question: At the time of the bodhisattva's training on the path, some of the time you spend working with relative bodhicitta, and with cultivating love and compassion and all these things. Then some of the time you are working on training your mind in cultivating emptiness. What I'm wondering is, when you are actually training in this path, how much time does the bodhisattva spend on each? Do you alternate from one to the other? Would you spend so many months intensively working on cultivating loving-kindness and compassion, and then so many months focusing on the cultivation of emptiness? How does a bodhisattva actually practice these things?

Rinpoche: Actually, it is a little misleading to take what it says in the text literally. Bodhisattvas do not *cultivate* absolute bodhicitta. They cultivate relative bodhicitta, and the result is absolute bodhicitta. They cultivate relative bodhicitta with recognition of where they are headed, but they do not actually have to practice them separately because relative bodhicitta is a method that leads to the discovery of absolute bodhicitta. The process of the path consists of gathering the two accumulations and removing the two obscurations. That is done in a strict mahayana context. In other words, when you are strictly concerned with bodhicitta *per se*, that is done through the cultivation of relative bodhicitta. Through cultivating love, compassion, and bodhicitta, there gradually emerges the direct experience that all things are like magical illusions, that things lack inherent existence, and so on, which is a result of that cultivation.

Question: Could you please elaborate on the stanza that says, "Whatever appears, all of this, is your mind."

Rinpoche: First you have to understand the meaning of this term "appearance," which is the same word that is also sometimes translated as "projection." Sometimes it means "experience" and sometimes even "illumination." Because of ignorance, because we do not recognize the nature of our minds, we are bewildered. Because of its cyclic quality we call that bewilderment "samsara," which literally means "circling." What appears to us within that bewilderment is "I," "you," "happiness," "suffering," and so on. All of these imputed qualities and characteristics are relative designations, in the sense that they are all imputations relative to something else. There is very little that could not possibly

85

appear to us; all sorts of things might appear to us. But *whatever* appears to us, whatever we experience, comes from our own mind. All of these imputations — of self, other, and all of that — are just that; they are imputations. Because they are imputations, they come from the mind. They do not exist outside. If you look at this mind that makes all these imputations, if you look at the nature of that mind, then you see that in itself, from the very beginning, it has always been beyond conceptual apprehension. When you look at that mind directly, there is nothing there that can be said to be something or nothing. If you recognize that, then you therefore recognize that the imputation of true or inherent existence to external objects and so on, is unnecessary and a function of bewilderment. Thus to the extent that you recognize that, you will never again generate this false imputation of true existence either to apprehended objects (appearances), or to the apprehending cognition (the mind).

Question: This is in reference to the verse about cultivating the meditative state of even placement. As I understand it, ordinary individuals like myself do not really have access to such a state of mind. We can not really give rise to this even placement. Therefore, how should I work with this type of instruction since I am an ordinary individual?

Rinpoche: It is not impossible that you could experience that, because it is always there. It has always been there. Actually, the reason we are ignorant of it, the reason we do not recognize it, is because it is right there. It is too close to us, and therefore it can not be grasped by objectification. In some liturgies it says, "All beings from the very beginning have been of the nature of a buddha, but are bewildered simply through not knowing that. I generate the bodhicitta of the recognition of things as they are." You are simply trying to see things as they are. If and when what impedes that experience is removed, then it will be obvious. It will be revealed. For example, we can not see someone else's body because they have clothes on. When the clothes are all gone, then you will see them, because there is nothing in the way. When your kleshas and so forth are all removed, then buddha nature, or absolute bodhicitta — it has many names that all mean the same thing — will be directly experienced.

Question: Does that mean that an ordinary person could have a partial recognition of this?

Rinpoche: There could be an experience of it, but not a full realization. The problem is that experiences are untrustworthy because they vanish like mist or rainbows.

(END OF QUESTIONS AND ANSWERS)

Thus far, Ngülchu Thogme's explanation of the path of the greater individual (a bodhisattva) has discussed the generation of bodhicitta and then meditation on the two bodhicittas, relative and absolute. The third and last section on this topic is about the bodhisattva's training in the observances connected with the two bodhicittas. This has five sections. The first is cultivating the six perfections; the second is training in the four things taught in the sutras; the third is training in abandoning mental afflictions; fourth is training in accomplishment of benefit for others through the possession of mindfulness and alertness; and fifth is training in the dedication of virtue to perfect awakening.

The first of these has six parts, corresponding to each of the six perfections. The first of these, the cultivation of generosity, which is the first of the perfections, is described in the twenty-fifth stanza: "If it is necessary for those who wish to attain awakening to give away even their bodies, then what need is there to say that all external possessions must at some time be given away. It is therefore the practice of bodhisattvas to give generously without any hope for repayment or a ripening." ("Ripening" means a personal benefit of any kind, even spiritual.)

As we find by studying the previous lives of the Buddha, a bodhisattva engaged in the accomplishment of buddhahood or perfect awakening must time after time give away parts of their body, various limbs and so on, and sometimes even their entire body and therefore their life, in order to benefit others. If such tremendous or difficult acts of generosity are routinely necessary for someone endeavoring to attain buddhahood, then what need is there to say that you must be ready to give away anything else as well. Therefore, to say the least, it is necessary to cultivate the practice of generosity from the beginning. This practice of generosity must be done in a way that is free from hope of some kind of payback. For example, if you hope to acquire in this life some kind of advantage through that generosity, such as thinking, "If I give this to them now, they will give me more later," or "If I give this to them, I'll acquire such and such reputation and such and such advantages." We need to be free from that kind of hope. We also need to be free from expecting advantages in future lives. In order to be pure, the practice of the perfection of generosity needs to be free from even the hope for the accumulation of good karma leading to mundane prosperity in future lives, such as thinking, "As a karmic result of this generosity I'll be wealthy in future lives." In short, the practice of generosity of a bodhisattva is done entirely for the benefit of the other beings to whom they give generously.

This generosity, which includes giving up the virtue accumulated through the act of generosity, is of three types. First there is material generosity, which is giving, as appropriate, external things that are necessary or beneficial to others. The second is the generosity of protection, which mainly means saving the lives of beings by protecting them from certain death and from other dangers as well. Third is the generosity of Dharma. This means that, with the understanding that it is your work to establish all beings who fill space (all of whom have been your mothers) in the state of perfect buddhahood, as appropriate and in accordance with your ability, you offer those beings access to Dharma. All these generosities are cultivated by bodhisattvas with the intention that the virtue they accumulate in doing so is also offered to beings.

The second of the six perfections is morality, or moral discipline. This is explained in the twenty-sixth stanza. It says, "If without morality you cannot accomplish your own benefit, to wish to accomplish benefit for others without morality is a joke. It is therefore the practice of bodhisattvas to preserve moral discipline that is free from the craving for further existence."

What is pointed out here is that the preservation of morality, which means keeping whatever moral commitments you have undertaken, is an absolute prerequisite for being reborn in higher realms, never mind helping others or even your own liberation. If you do not undertake and preserve moral commitments, not only will you not progress towards liberation, you will definitely be reborn in lower realms. Therefore, to violate moral commitments and to claim to be trying to benefit others is ridiculous. It is completely impossible. In fact, you could not even progress yourself. Thus a bodhisattva, whose entire intention is to do only that which is beneficial to others, will therefore keep flawless moral discipline.

The special feature of the morality of bodhisattvas is that it is not undertaken merely in order to attain a higher rebirth. It is said, of course, that the only cause of superior rebirth is flawless morality. However, a bodhisattva does not undertake morality merely to secure a higher rebirth. That is what is meant by being "free from the craving for further existence." They do not undertake it only for their own liberation; it is undertaken entirely in order to be able to benefit others most effectively.

With regard to the different motivations one might have for keeping flawless morality, there is a story about a series of events that occurred during the Buddha's lifetime. The Buddha had a close relative who, according to some accounts, was the Buddha's cousin and therefore Ananda's brother, and according to some other accounts was Ananda's cousin and therefore the Buddha's younger brother. I think he may have been the Buddha's younger brother. In any case, he was a member of the Sakya clan and quite closely related to the Buddha. His name was Nanda, which means "Delightful." (This is not to be confused with Ananda, which means "Totally Delightful.") To make the names even more confusing, Nanda's wife was known as Nandi, which is the feminine form of "Delightful."

Nanda was someone with enormous manifest potential, and the Buddha realized that if he could somehow strategically get Nanda to attain arhatship in that life, he would be of tremendous benefit to other members of the sangha and to beings in general. The context of this, of course, is basic Buddhist monastic tradition, so don't be offended by these events. The problem was that in order to attain arhatship, of course, you have to be a monk or nun. And Nanda was very, very attached — obsessively attached — to his wife. This was not hard to understand because his wife was an extraordinary person. She was extremely intelligent, extremely kind, and also very beautiful. Therefore Nanda was always in conflict because he had a desire to become the Buddha's student, but he also did not want to get involved with being a monk, so he was kind of waffling back and forth.

One day the Buddha was begging and went to Nanda's door. Nanda answered the door and his wife wanted to know who was there, and he replied, "It's the Buddha. I'm going to offer him some food." He offered the Buddha food, but then the Buddha handed him his begging bowl and said, "Come with me. Walk back with me to where I'm staying." Nandi said, "You can go with him, but you must be back by the time this is dry," and she licked the hem of her skirt. So Nanda went with the Buddha, but once he got to the place where the sangha was living, he felt inspired and requested to be ordained as a monk. The Buddha consented, and he was ordained. But he wasn't completely in one world or the other, so even after he was ordained, having abruptly left his wife, he was thinking about her all the time. He couldn't even perform shamata practice because his mind

90

was full of the image of his wife. He began drawing pictures of his wife on rocks. The Buddha, of course, became concerned about this. He said to the other members of the sangha, "We are all here for one reason, which is that we want to obtain liberation, except for my brother, Nanda, who is still really obsessed with things of this life. So give him some space."

Finally, it got to the point where the Buddha decided he had to do something, so he took Nanda to the top of a mountain where there was a colony of monkeys. Among them was a female monkey that was particularly deformed. He said to Nanda, "Who looks better to you, this monkey or your wife?" Nanda replied, "I don't know what you're talking about. My wife is a thousand times more beautiful than this monkey!" The Buddha didn't say anything and they went back.

On another day the Buddha, through his miraculous powers, took Nanda to the realm of the gods, and Nanda saw many magnificently beautiful goddesses. The Buddha asked Nanda, "Who is more attractive, these goddesses or your wife?" Nanda said, "How can you even ask? These goddesses are a thousand times more beautiful than my wife." The Buddha didn't say anything, and they went back.

After that, Nanda really became a good monk, because he decided that he did not want to live with his wife anymore. He wanted to be a perfect monk so that he could be reborn in that god realm and enjoy the company of those goddesses. Thus his behavior changed and he seemed to be at peace and was practicing intensively. The Buddha, however, was aware that his fundamental intention was still really the same. He still was trying to have a good time.

So next the Buddha took him to a hell realm. When he was there, Nanda saw all sorts of cauldrons filled with molten metal, and beings being plunged into them, and all kinds of nasty things like that. At a certain point he saw one empty cauldron. He asked the demons who were guarding the cauldron, "Why is this cauldron empty?" They said, "The brother of the Buddha, whose name is Nanda, is a perfect monk. As a result of that he is going to be reborn in the realm of the gods, and for a long time enjoy the company of delightful goddesses. However, when he has used up his merit in that way and he dies, he will be reborn here. He will have our company instead." At that point, Nanda started to feel that he was about to fall into the molten metal in the cauldron. He became completely terrified, and after returning, had no desire for any kind of positive rebirth. He only wanted out of samsara. Thereafter he became an arhat, a great teacher, and benefited many people.

This shows that you could behave perfectly on the outside, but for different reasons. The point of this story is that there has to be a pure motivation, not simply the wish to achieve a higher rebirth.

Now the actual practice of morality, which is to be practiced with that motivation, has three aspects. The first is the morality which is abstention from wrongdoing. That is the fundamental aspect of morality. Second, there is the morality of vigorously accomplishing that which is good, in other words, the gathering of virtue. Third is the moral discipline of conscientiously benefiting others.

The third perfection, which is dealt with in the twenty-seventh stanza, is the perfection of patience. It says in the text, "For a bodhisattva who wishes to enjoy or achieve virtue, abusers are like a precious treasure. Therefore, it is the practice of bodhisattvas to cultivate patience that is without anger or aggression."

It is said that patience is the supreme austerity, just as aggression is the strongest wrongdoing. It is also said that if nothing makes you angry, how can you exercise patience? Patience has to be exercised against resistance. The resistance is created by a situation that requires the exercise of patience. Without that your patience will not develop. The best situation, that which requires the most development of patience, is one in which someone else is abusing you. Thus while we would conventionally regard an abuser as something undesirable to be avoided at all costs, a bodhisattva sees it differently. For a bodhisattva who wishes to cultivate virtue, wishes to attain buddhahood, and therefore wishes to cultivate patience (which is an absolute necessity in order to attain buddhahood), an abusive situation is like a wish-fulfilling jewel. That is because it is an opportunity for them to cultivate tremendous patience. It is therefore the practice of bodhisattvas, when faced with the abuse of others, not to respond with aggression, but with delight and satisfaction.

The actual practice of patience has three aspects. First is the patience that thinks nothing of abuse. In other words, it means not making a big deal out of any situation, and not being affected or stirred by it. The second is the patience that is the acceptance of suffering. Third is the patience which is certainty about the Dharma, not being frightened by the profundities of Dharma, the inconceivable nature of things, and so forth.

The fourth of the six perfections is diligence or exertion. It is described in stanza twenty-eight as follows: "If even shravakas and pratyekabuddhas, who are endeavoring to accomplish only their own benefit, engage in diligence like that of someone whose head has caught fire, then it is all the more obvious that it must be a practice of bodhisattvas to engage in that diligence which is the source of all qualities that are of benefit to all beings."

Anyone who wishes to benefit themselves, either in the temporary sense of achieving higher rebirth, or in the ultimate sense of achieving full liberation, must practice with diligence in order to achieve either of these aims. In particular shravakas and pratyekabuddhas, who are endeavoring to attain the cessation of an arhat and are not primarily concerned with benefiting other sentient beings, practice with a diligence that is like that of someone whose head has caught fire. The meaning of this image is that if your head

93

catches fire you are not going to procrastinate! You will do everything you can to extinguish the fire immediately. If even shravakas and pratyekabuddhas practice with such ferocious diligence, then how much more necessary must it be for bodhisattvas, who are endeavoring to accomplish not merely their own personal liberation, but the liberation of all beings, to practice with ferocious diligence. The motivation for the diligence of bodhisattvas is that force of bodhicitta, which is their motivation for the entire path. That is a stronger motivation than the desire for liberation in and of itself. Therefore the diligence of bodhisattvas is even greater and even stronger.

The diligence that bodhisattvas cultivate has three aspects. The first is the armorlike diligence, which is the fundamental intention to be diligent. The second is the *application* of that fundamental intention, which is the actual accomplishment or gathering of virtue. Third, there is the diligence that is the accomplishment of benefit for other beings. Thus the three parts are: (1) the intention; (2) the application of that intention in practice; and then (3) the actual benefiting of other beings.

The fifth perfection is meditation, or meditative stability, which is described in stanza twenty-nine as follows: "Knowing that the mental afflictions are conquered by a vipasyana which is fully endowed with shamata, it is the practice of bodhisattvas to cultivate a meditation that completely transcends the four formless realms."

The perfection of meditation, or dhyana, has two aspects in its authentic form. The first is shamata, or tranquility, which is defined as a mind that is one-pointedly focused on a virtuous object. The second is vipasyana, or insight, which is the realization of emptiness. This insight, of course, is what really conquers the mental afflictions, because they are destroyed or eradicated by the realization of emptiness. This realization of emptiness cannot occur in the absence of the support or environment of shamata, however. Therefore true meditative stability is a vipasyana that is founded upon

94

or endowed with an authentic state of shamata, a mind that is one-pointedly focused on virtue. Through the integration of those two, then the mental afflictions, including fundamental ignorance, can be eradicated. Because the two aspects of shamata and vipasyana are present, the meditative stability of a bodhisattva transcends the meditative absorptions of the four formless realms, such as limitless space and so forth. There are four such absorptions, and those absorptions are basically profound states of shamata without that vipasyana which is the realization of emptiness. Bodhisattvas cultivate in their meditation the vipasyana that brings about transcendence of the extreme of existence — that is, a further involvement in samsara, including the samsaric absorptions of the formless realms. At the same time, they always keep the compassionate motivation of bodhicitta, so although they bring about the cessation of samsara, they do not abide in cessation alone, as do arhats. Therefore, they transcend the extreme of tranquility, or cessation. In that way, their realization of emptiness (which is assisted by shamata) is inseparable from their compassion and bodhicitta. Through such a meditative absorption they avoid the two extremes of samsara and cessation.

The practice of meditative absorption has three aspects. They are: (1) the meditation that abides in bliss; (2) the meditation that is the actual accomplishment of qualities; and (3) the meditation which benefits beings.

The sixth and last of the six perfections is prajna, or knowledge. This is described in the thirtieth stanza, which says, "Without knowledge, one cannot attain perfect awakening through the other five perfections. It is therefore the practice of bodhisattvas to cultivate a knowledge endowed with skillful means that does not conceptualize the three aspects."

The idea here is that knowledge, which is defined in the context of the perfections as the knowledge that is the realization of emptiness, is like the eyes that inform or bring insight to the practice or method of the other five perfections. In the absence of such a realization of emptiness, the

95

other five perfections will not bring about full enlightenment, or buddhahood. Thus when bodhisattvas practice, the substance of their practice is skillful means or method, which means enacting all of the articulations or manifestations of bodhicitta as the foregoing five perfections, with the affect or motivation of great compassion. However, when they implement these methods or these expressions of compassion and bodhicitta, they do so without reification of the three aspects of that implementation.

The three aspects are: (1) that which is being cultivated; (2) that which, or who, is cultivating it; and (3) the manner and result of that cultivation. For example, in the case of generosity, it would be the person who is giving, that which is given, and the recipient. Therefore the prajna aspect is that each of the five methods, or foregoing perfections, is accompanied by a realization of the emptiness, or lack of true existence, of the three aspects of the situation of those perfections. Thus bodhisattvas cultivate the virtuous practices within, or accompanied by, the realization of emptiness. The presence of the sixth perfection causes the other five virtues to become true perfections.

In detail, the sixth perfection, prajna, can be divided into three, like the others. This can be done in different ways. Here, they are categorized as (1) mundane knowledge; (2) supermundane knowledge, i.e., the realization of the selflessness of persons; and (3) great supermundane knowledge, which is the realization of the emptiness of everything.

The second of the five trainings of the two bodhicittas is the cultivation of the four things taught in the sutras. The first of these is examining our own defects and abandoning them; the second is abandoning criticism of bodhisattvas; the third is abandoning attachment to the homes and property of patrons; and the fourth is abandoning harsh speech.

The first of these, abandoning our own defects through becoming aware of them, is described in the thirty-first stanza, which says: "If you do not examine your own bewilderment, you could become someone with the appearance of a practitioner who is engaged in the practice of non-Dharma. It is therefore the practice of bodhisattvas to continually examine their own bewilderment, and having detected it, then abandon it."

If you are practicing Dharma, especially the mahayana, you need to continually examine your own mind to detect your own self-deception, defects, and bewilderment. If you do not do that it is very easy for your external appearance of involvement with practice to remain purely external. The reality will be that you will come to have an outer shell of Dharma, and an inner kernel of kleshas. As was said by Jamgön Kongtrül Lodrö Thaye, a person can look like a practitioner but have a completely untamed mind that secretly harbors all the kleshas. You could have the appearance of being learned, noble in behavior, excellent in disposition, and really not have any of these qualities on the inside. Without examining your own defects, you will not be aware of them. You could have a heap of defects as big as Mt. Meru and still think that you are a great practitioner. People can not tell what is inside your mind, they can only see your behavior, and you could fool everyone around you. Everybody around you might think that you are really a great practitioner because you know how to act, how to fake it. As a result, you have a further problem: because you appear to be a practitioner while inside you are not really taming your mind at all, you start to use, initially unconsciously, the appearance and social position of being a practitioner in order to accomplish mundane ambitions that are not Dharmic, and which actually go against the Dharma. That would include doing things such as harming or subduing those you regard as enemies, helping those you regard as friends (in a biased or improper way), and so on. Therefore not examining your own defects is a big problem. It is therefore the practice of bodhisattvas to continually closely examine their own behavior, their own speech, their own minds, and — having detected a defect — do their best to get rid of it on the spot.

The second of the four things taught in the sutras is abandoning criticism of other bodhisattvas, which means other mahayana practitioners in general, and especially realized bodhisattvas. It says in stanza thirty-two, "If, under the power of mental afflictions, a mahayana practitioner proclaims the defects of another bodhisattva or mahayana practitioner, then the proclaimer becomes impaired (the proclaimer's virtue degenerates). It is therefore the practice of bodhisattvas not to proclaim the defects of those who have entered the mahayana."

This refers to situations where through the power of mental afflictions, especially jealousy, a mahayana practitioner bad-mouths another mahayana practitioner — proclaims their downfalls, the defects in their conduct, their general failings, and so on. And this only hurts the one who is broadcasting the faults, because they are acting out of jealousy. It is therefore the practice of bodhisattvas not to criticize other beings in general, and especially those who have entered any vehicle of Dharma, and most particularly the mahayana. In short it means to be careful with your speech — to control your speech. Essentially the point of this, which goes along with the previous stanza, is to be more concerned with your own defects than the defects of others.

The third thing taught in the sutras is to relinquish attachment to the homes and possessions of patrons. In the thirty-third stanza it says, "Because competition over service and acquisition causes the impairment of hearing, contemplation, and meditation, it is the practice of bodhisattvas to abandon attachment to the homes of friends, family, and patrons."

When practitioners are being benefited by a patron, who could be a friend, relative, or anyone who offers support, this can create a situation — if there is excessive involvement with the benefactor — leading to competition among practitioners for the patronage. That competition, obviously, goes against the grain of Dharma in general. When practitioners are involved with competing for the favor of patrons, they are less involved with what they are supposed to be doing, namely hearing the Dharma, thinking about it, and meditating. Therefore it is the practice of bodhisattvas to refrain from excessive attachment to, or dependence upon, the homes and wealth of those who support them.

Finally, the fourth thing taught in the sutras is to abandon harsh speech. In stanza thirty-four it says, "Since harsh words agitate the minds of others, and therefore cause one's bodhisattva conduct to degenerate, it is the practice of bodhisattvas to abandon harsh words that are unpleasant for others."

When we do not pay attention to our own defects through carelessness, for example, we may become angry and carelessly speak harshly to others and agitate them. This can hurt their feelings and make them angry. Therefore bodhisattvas and those practicing the mahayana should speak gently. They should speak appropriately, and in a manner that is easy on the ears and that sounds right to those who are hearing it. When you speak carelessly and hurt someone's feelings, this is obviously going directly against the whole purpose of the bodhisattva path — which is not to cause suffering, but to bring beings happiness. It is therefore a great downfall for a bodhisattva to do so. Therefore bodhisattvas abandon harsh words, which means that they think carefully about what sort of language and what sort of things to say that will actually be pleasant and appropriate for that person. Watching one's speech is very important. In general it is said, "When alone, look at your mind; when in company, look at what you are saying."

The third observance of the two bodhicittas is training in abandoning the kleshas, which is described in the thirty-fifth stanza: "Since it is difficult to reverse the kleshas, even with their antidotes or remedies once one has become habituated to them, it is the practice of bodhisattvas to crush mental afflictions such as attachment as soon as they arise, having grasped the weapon of mindfulness and alertness, which is the remedy."

99

The point of this is that if you allow mental afflictions, such as attachment, aversion, apathy, pride, and jealousy, simply to arise as they arise, without immediately applying the remedy — which is to say, if you do not recognize the arising of a klesha with alertness, through the steady or constant application of mindfulness — then the klesha, having arisen, will therefore increase in power and become even more entrenched in your mind, making it progressively more difficult to remove. It is therefore the practice of bodhisattvas, as soon as a mental affliction such as attachment arises, to crush it, and get rid of it on the spot with the sharp weapon of alertness and the faculty of mindfulness. What is meant by mindfulness here is not forgetting what is to be undertaken and what is to be avoided. Thus it means the steady recollection of not wishing to undertake kleshas, but to avoid them. Alertness, which ensues upon mindfulness, means knowing what is happening with your body, speech, and mind as it is happening. Mindfulness and alertness together are like a sharp weapon that can cut through on the spot — or as the text says, crush — the kleshas as they arise. Continually holding that weapon, bodhisattvas wait for the arising of a klesha and deal with it right away without procrastination.

The fourth training or observance of the two bodhicittas is training in the accomplishment of benefit for others through the application of these same two faculties, mindfulness (or recollection) and alertness (or awareness). This is described in the thirty-sixth stanza of the central thirty-seven, which says, "In brief, whatever activity you are engaged in, and whatever the state of your mind, to continually accomplish benefit for others through possessing mindfulness and alertness is the practice of bodhisattvas."

This stanza is a summary of the first thirty-five, and it points out what is common to all thirty-five stanzas. If all of those practices are summarized into one point, it is this: to continually maintain an unimpaired faculty of mindfulness and therefore an unimpaired faculty of alertness in all situations.

This applies to whatever you are doing, and no matter what is going on in your mind, no matter how you feel, and whether you are in a virtuous or positive state of mind or an unvirtuous or negative state of mind. Specifically it means being constantly mindful of your intention to only benefit others and not to harm them, and therefore being alert about what you are doing. In that way what you do actually *is* only of benefit to others, and you continually succeed in accomplishing that benefit. That is the extremely precious or most important root of all of these practices of bodhisattvas.

Finally, the thirty-seventh stanza explains the fifth training of the two bodhicittas, which is dedicating all one's virtue to perfect awakening in order to be able to liberate others. It says, "It is the practice of bodhisattvas to dedicate all of the virtues accomplished through diligently engaging in those practices to full awakening in order to be able to remove the sufferings of infinite sentient beings, and to do that dedication within the knowledge that is free from conceptualization of the three aspects."

It is the practice of bodhisattvas to dedicate all of the virtue they accumulate through their great diligence—which is here defined as a joyous entrance into virtue (the definition of diligence is delight in virtue)—to the attainment of perfect awakening, so they can, as quickly and effectively as possible, liberate all beings without exception from all suffering and establish them in enlightenment. They dedicate not only the virtues they have accumulated up to that point, but the virtues they are accumulating as they dedicate, and the virtues they will accumulate in the future, and in addition, the virtues of other beings as well. Furthermore, their dedication is done without a reification of the dedicator, the dedicated, and the recipients. This means they do not erroneously conceive of the virtue, themselves, or the sentient beings to whom they are dedicating it as having true or inherent existence. That is the special feature of the dedication of a bodhisattva, which is embraced by that knowledge of the emptiness of the three aspects, and is dedicated to the perfect awakening of all beings.

This completes the description of the practices of the greater individual, which is the third part of the main practice and the second part of the central body of the text. Remember that there were seven stanzas on the preliminaries and thirty on the main practice (which includes one stanza on the path of the lesser individual, one on the path of an intermediate individual, and then twenty-eight on the path of a greater individual). Those thirty-seven stanzas were preceded, you will remember, by two stanzas, one of homage and one which was a statement of intention. We have now gone over these thirty-nine stanzas. The third part is the conclusion of the text, which is called "excellence in the end."

This has five parts, which are four more stanzas and then the colophon, which is not versified. The five parts are: (1) explaining how this was composed and for whose benefit; (2) demonstrating that this is an unmistaken explanation of these practices; (3) a request for patience in connection with an expression of modesty; (4) a dedication of the virtue of this composition to awakening; and (5) the colophon, which is in a form that is called "fourfold excellence."

The first of these is the fortieth stanza, which says, "Following the teachings of the holy ones, which are explanations of that which was taught in the sutras, tantras, and shastras, I have set forth these thirty-seven practices of bodhisattvas for the benefit of those who wish to train in the path of a bodhisattva."

The first part explains that the source of these teachings is the original teachings of the Buddha in the sutras and tantras in general, and in particular the mahayana sutras and the shastras (commentaries on the sutras), which clarify or set forth their meaning and intention. In particular the author is saying he has presented these teachings as they were expounded and further clarified by the great forefathers of the lineage, especially the great teachers of the Kadampa tradition of Lord Atisha and his heart son Geshe Dromtönpa. In short, this teaching came down to Thogme Zangpo, the author, from his teachers and his masters. In other words, it is the Buddha's teachings as expressed in the Indian commentaries, as transmitted by the masters of the Kadampa lineage, on down to Thogme's own teacher. Coming from that lineage, it has been gathered into these thirty-seven practices or aspects of the bodhisattva path, set forth here for the benefit of those who have the good fortune to wish to practice this path.

The second part of the conclusion, which is stanza forty-one, is the demonstration that the explanation of these practices is unmistaken and reliable. Thogme writes, "Because I am unintelligent and untrained, there is no composition here to delight the learned. However, because I have relied upon the sutras and the teachings or speech of the holy ones, I think that this is an unmistaken explanation of the practices of bodhisattvas."

Of course, his statement that he is unintelligent and untrained is not literally true. He is saying this as a demonstration of the need to be modest, which is in keeping with the general intention and tone of the text. Nevertheless, the meaning of what he says is, "I, who have composed this text, am unintelligent. That is to say, I was born with little intelligence and I have little knowledge, so therefore there is nothing here that is going to especially delight the learned, knowledgeable, and intelligent. Especially there are no extraordinary feats of composition. However, I would like to point out that this text does not contain anything that I have simply made up myself or anything that is incorrect. Because it relies entirely upon the Buddha's teachings in the sutras and the teachings of the holy individuals who have followed those teachings, I think it is an accurate and therefore reliable description of the practices of bodhisattvas."

The third part of the conclusion, which is stanza forty-two, is a further expression of modesty and a request for patience. He has just said, "I think this is correct," but then he says,

"However, because it is difficult for someone as unintelligent as myself to fathom the vast practices or conduct of bodhisattvas, should there be any contradictions or disconnectedness — in short, any flaws — I request the patience of the holy ones with this."

He is saying that although he thinks his explanation of the practices is reliable, nevertheless because the conduct and practices of bodhisattvas are almost infinite in scope and profundity, like a vast ocean, then how could someone as unintelligent as himself (as unintelligent as he is claiming to be) fathom them? Because of that, there might be some kind of contradiction between one stanza and another, or maybe some lack of connectedness in the composition of the text. If there are such defects, he requests the patience of the holy ones with this. This is included because it is customary, and in order to demonstrate the need for modesty. It is also a way of showing the true profundity of the bodhisattva practices so that we do not think they are shallow or too easy.

The final stanza, the forty-third, is the fourth part of the conclusion. It is the dedication of the virtue of this composition to awakening. It says, "Through the virtue which has arisen from that composition, may all beings, through the generation of the supreme bodhicittas, relative and absolute, attain the supreme awakening that is beyond both samsara and nirvana."

The meaning of this stanza brings us back to the homage at the beginning, which was an homage to Avalokiteshvara as transcending the two extremes. In this last stanza, Ngülchu Thogme is saying that through whatever virtue has arisen through this composition, may all beings attain the supreme awakening that avoids the two extremes of samsara and nirvana. That awakening is expressed here as the state of the protector or Bodhisattva Avalokiteshvara. It is an aspiration that beings attain this through generating the two bodhicittas. In the case of absolute bodhicitta, it is the manifestation of that knowledge which is the direct realization of emptiness. With relative bodhicitta, it is the wish to attain perfect awakening for the benefit of others, motivated by great compassion. Thus there is the aspiration that beings may quickly attain these two states of mind, and in that way through the supreme knowledge of emptiness which is absolute bodhicitta, may they transcend samsara. In other words, may they not abide in the extreme of cyclic existence. As well, through the generation of relative bodhicitta, the nature of which is great compassion, may they transcend the extreme of the cessation of an arhat. In that way, attaining the supreme awakening which does not abide in either samsara or cessation, may they exhibit that supreme conduct which is skillful and which is the nature of non-conceptual compassion. Each being having attained this, may they thereafter exhibit this activity until all other beings have attained this state as well, just like the protector Arya Avalokiteshvara.

Finally, the fifth part of the conclusion is the prose colophon to the text, which says, "This was written for the benefit of myself and others by the monk Thogme, who teaches scripture and reasoning in the Precious Cave of Mercury." (This is the name of the place where he resided.) In that way it shows the four excellences, which are: (1) why the text was written; (2) for whom it was written; (3) by whom it was written; and (4) where it was written.

QUESTIONS AND ANSWERS

Question: Could you please define what you mean by "reification?"

Translator: The word I'm translating with "reification" means to impute reality to something that does not possess it.

Question: I have a question going back to verse thirty-three, which is about relinquishing attachment to homes and possessions of patrons. Can you speak more about how that works with relatives, family, and people close to you?

Rinpoche: Basically that is about taking things for granted. Although it mentions family in the root text and commentary, it typically refers to a situation where you, as a practitioner, are dealing with possessions that are not yours. In a family, depending upon the degree of immediate family, distant family, and so on, there may or may not be a distinction between the possessions of different members. For example, sometimes the home of one's parents is considered to be the home of the children as well, and sometimes it is not. Basically, in a family context, whether or not this problem can occur depends upon the degree of familial connection.

The primary concern of that stanza is a situation where you get used to having and using something that is not in fact yours, and you start to take it for granted and regard it to be — and treat it as though it were — your possession. This happens most with patronage situations, but it can also happen in friendships, and also, as you say, within the family. For example, if you are using the possessions of a friend or a patron for whatever length of time, when you start you have a clear awareness that these belong to someone else. You think, "Well, I mustn't get this dirty, I mustn't use all of this up, and I must keep it in the right place." Over time you get so used to having unlimited access to whatever it

106

is, a home or possession, that you are no longer concerned about whether you get it dirty or not, because you forget that you are ever going to return it to somebody else. You are no longer concerned about using it up, and in fact, you are willing to sell it, never mind keeping it in the right place.

Another problem that is addressed by the text concerns situations where there is competition for patronage. For example, two people wish to be supported by the same patron and are worrying about who is getting more support. It could also be the case that two patrons wish to support someone and are competing for who is giving more support. This can be the cause either of resentment for having to give more support, or resentment for not being able to give more support. In short, patronage can lead to a lot of competition and to the simple situation of taking things for granted.

Question: I wanted to ask about verse thirty-two, which is connected with abandoning criticism of other bodhisattvas. Is it ever appropriate, under special circumstances, if you feel that there are individuals who could be harming others, and you feel that to benefit someone else you should let them know about this person's activity?

Rinpoche: The text is not saying that you should never criticize other practitioners. If appropriate, you can and should do so when it is necessary in order to prevent a situation of harm or abuse, as you said. However, you should not do so out of dislike or jealousy.

Question: Could you talk a little bit more about stanza thirty-one, which talks about the necessity of examining our own bewilderment? Sometimes I think I am confused about what my motivation is. Also, I'm not sure I understand how to look at or observe my state of confusion, and how to gain greater clarity.

Rinpoche: You need to be particularly clear about what the intention of this text is, what it is actually focusing on. Since it is basically a text on the practice of bodhicitta, it is primarily concerned with maintaining the pure intention that anything you do is done to benefit others. In that stanza in particular, when it talks about always examining your own bewilderment, it is not so much saying that you need to be obsessively worried about how confused you are and how bewildered you are, in the sense of basic ignorance. That is something you work out slowly through practice and through working with your personal teacher. What it is talking about here is when you are involved in a situation where you are supposedly doing something to help others. You have to be very clear that you are not being self-deceptive about your motivation for doing it—that you are not doing something to help yourself in the guise of helping or teaching somebody else.

If you study this stanza together with stanza thirty-six, you will understand the point of it. That stanza says, "In brief, whatever activity you are engaged in, and whatever the state of your mind, to continually accomplish benefit for others through possessing mindfulness and alertness is the practice of bodhisattvas." In other words, it means always to be mindful of your intention such that you are really, genuinely trying to help others. That is because we could give the appearance of trying to help others, without actually having that attitude.

Question: I seem to remember one of the points saying that the bodhisattva actually seeks abuse. Couldn't that be misinterpreted?

Rinpoche: No, I did not say that, and the text does not say that. What was said was that a bodhisattva would take the attitude of welcoming and learning from such situations. Welcoming something when it comes along is very different from seeking it out. We really do not have to seek out situations where people do not treat us well. Those situations are pretty easy to come by! When they do arise, if we can work with them as the text teaches us, that transforms such situations into wish-fulfilling jewels.

THE SIX PERFECTIONS

To begin our discussion of the six perfections, it would be good to bring to mind what was said earlier about bodhicitta, the mind of awakening. We said that if the merit of bodhicitta had form, it would fill the entire universe and in fact would be even larger than that. This image represents the fact that the merit of meditating on bodhicitta, which means cultivating loving-kindness and compassion for all beings, is immeasurable. As you come to understand bodhicitta, you will see that it is the most essential and important aspect of Dharma.

Bodhicitta has two aspects: relative and absolute. Relative bodhicitta is also divided into two aspects, which are known as aspiration bodhicitta and implementation bodhicitta. The six perfections are the trainings or practices of this implementation bodhicitta.

Even more meritorious than the cultivation of the aspiration bodhicitta of loving-kindness and compassion is the cultivation of the training of the six perfections, which is the same training and implementation bodhicitta that has been engaged in by all the buddhas and bodhisattvas in the past. The six perfections are generosity, morality, patience, diligence, meditative stability, and knowledge.

Since the six perfections are the trainings of implementation bodhicitta, then this training must be preceded by the generation of aspiration bodhicitta. What is aspiration bodhicitta? It is the generation of the attitude or thought that, "Just as all of the previous buddhas and bodhisattvas have generated the intention to attain supreme awakening, in exactly the way that they did, I generate this intention." Implementation bodhicitta goes beyond this pure and perfect intention of aspiration bodhicitta. It means actually engaging in the practice of the six perfections, in short, of all of the practices that have been done by all buddhas and bodhisattvas of the past in order to attain awakening. These practices are the means to attain the awakening for which you have aspired. The difference between aspiration and implementation bodhicitta is therefore said to be like the difference between wishing to go somewhere and actually going on the journey to that place.

In general, the six perfections are the practice of implementation bodhicitta. In particular, among the six perfections, the one that is the most important is patience. In practice, it is only possible to work on developing patience in the presence of something that could anger us. Without something to potentially make us angry, there is no possible way we can practice or exercise patience. Thus in situations of family life, work, and things such as working with a Dharma center, we have a great opportunity to cultivate patience.

Let's consider briefly why the perfections are called that. What is perfect about them? The first of the six is the perfection of generosity. It is called the perfection of generosity because from the actual act of generosity itself, all the way until the arising of the complete result of that generosity, the entire process is sealed with the non-conceptualization of the giver, the gift, and the recipient. This absence of conceptualization of these three aspects is what makes this virtue of generosity what is called the transcendent virtue or perfection of generosity. Therefore, when we speak, for example, of the perfection of generosity, we are using the term of the cause, "generosity," together with the term for the result, "perfection." In the same way, the names of each of the perfections, such as the perfection of morality, of patience, and so on, link the cause, which is the particular act, with the result, which is the transcendent virtue or perfection. As we go along, we will discuss in more depth what is meant by the non-conceptualization of the three aspects, since it is very closely tied to the meaning of the sixth perfection, that of knowledge or *prajna*.

Among the six perfections, the first to be considered in sequence is generosity, and generosity has three aspects: material generosity, dharmic generosity, and the giving of protection. The first of these, material generosity, also has three varieties, which are giving, great giving, and utmost giving. There is one thing about this act of giving that needs to be understood from the beginning. Whether you are giving something large or something small, the act of generosity cannot be performed within the context of having a great hope for some kind of payback or personal profit. For example, if you give someone one dollar with the hope that you will acquire a good reputation or a good name in the community, or in the hope that at some point in the future they will give you two dollars, this is not the pure practice of generosity. Generosity, whether it is great or small, must be done without any hope for personal benefit. It must be done entirely out of the hope of benefiting the recipient, making them happy, and alleviating their particular suffering, whether it is poverty or any other suffering.

The first of these three types of material generosity, which is simply called giving, is giving something material that can be quite small. For example, it could be a bowl of food or a cup of tea. It is important to understand that provided your motivation for giving is pure, the size of the gift itself is basically irrelevant. In a traditional Buddhist practice called "the confession of downfalls," it is said that the virtue of giving even a mouthful of food to an animal can be a tremendous act of virtue if your motivation is pure.

Furthermore, by making use of the profound meditations and mantras that have been taught by the skillful and compassionate Buddha, you can actually transform a very small material offering into something that will be perceived by its recipients as something tremendously large. For example, by consecrating one drop of water or one grain with a mantra known as the sky-treasury mantra or others like it, you can cause it to be experienced by numberless recipients, such as animals and especially hungry ghosts, as an inexhaustible treasury of desirable offerings which fulfill their every

Bardor Tulku Rinpoche

need, as multitudinous as the grains of sand in the river Ganges. Furthermore, those recipients to whom it is dedicated will all receive the offering equally, without some getting it and others missing it and so on.

In connection with this type of generosity, there is a practice that is traditionally done in the evenings which is called the burnt offering or *sur*. There are two types of *sur* offerings. The first is called the *karsur*, or white burnt offering, in which case the offerings consist of grain, yogurt, milk, and sometimes pieces of silk or other cloth that are burnt or singed in a fire. The characteristic of the *karsur* is that no meat whatsoever is used. The other type of *sur* offering is called the *marsur* or red burnt offering, in which the ingredients are the same as above but with the addition of meat. The ritual that is recited in connection with the burning of the offerings is designed to consecrate them so that the smoke of the offerings can actually be received by the intended recipients. In the case of the *karsur*, the primary recipients, those who are especially benefited by it, are the types of *pretas* (hungry ghosts) who move about through the human realm. Most of those pretas like what are called the "three whites and the three sweets," which are milk, yogurt, and butter, and sugar, molasses, and honey. The reason it is necessary to especially dedicate the offerings to these beings is that the nature of pretas is that they cannot receive anything that is not particularly dedicated to them. In the case of the *marsur*, the basic attitude is the same, but in that case the particular recipients are potentially spiteful or harmful spirits who would otherwise hurt you and others, and by receiving the offerings they are pleased and satisfied, and their spitefulness is alleviated. An essential part of this practice is the consecration of the practitioner through meditation on him or herself as Chenrezig, and the consecration of the offerings through the use of the various mantras such as the sky-treasury mantra and others.

The function of all of these elements coming together is that the intended beings not only receive physical satisfaction from receiving the offerings, but are benefited in other ways as well. Because the ritual contains the mantras of Chenrezig and other deities, it becomes not only material generosity but also the generosity of the Dharma. As well, since by satisfying these spirits you prevent them from harming other beings, then it also becomes the generosity of protection. Therefore the practice of *sur* is a complete practice of threefold generosity.

Whether the practice of *sur* uses an abbreviated or an extensive liturgy, in general the recipients of the *sur* offering consist of four classes of recipients, who are called the four guests or recipients. The first of these is the Three Jewels, who are recipients of veneration, and they are offered the first portion of the offering, which in their case is considered an offering and not a gift. The purpose of making this offering to them is that through doing so you accumulate a vast amount of merit.

The second is the protectors, who are the recipients who possess qualities, and the qualities that they possess are their ability to bestow protection upon you.

The third class of recipients are your karmic creditors — those beings to whom you owe some kind of karmic debt. This includes those who have spite toward you because of these karmic debts. These beings, who may be pretas or beings of other realms, are beings who wish to harm you and others. In large part, their wish to do so comes from the fact that in previous lives, the beings that they wish to harm have withheld food and clothing from them, or have actually stolen the necessities of life from them. They may also be beings to whom you incurred some kind of debt in a previous life that was never repaid. In short, these are beings that hold grudges, and they are the third category of recipients.

The fourth category is all sentient beings of the six realms in general. In this context they are called "the six realms, the recipients of compassion," because each and every being of the six realms undergoes the particular type of suffering that characterizes their particular realm, and they all are equally deserving of receiving your compassion.

In connection with this description of the *sur* or burnt offering, one thing has to be clarified. People often fail to make the necessary distinction between what is called the *sang* and what is called the *sur*, both of which tend to be referred to in English as a "fire puja." A *sang* means a cleansing offering. It is an offering of smoke, such as the smoke of juniper, and also the smoke of grains as well. Mainly, though, it is the smoke of juniper or other coniferous tree branches. This is done in order to cleanse the environment. *Sang* is generally done in the morning and rarely, if ever, in the evening. The principal idea of a *sang* or cleansing offering, is to enhance the prosperity or richness and purity of the environment or region in which it is done. Therefore it benefits not only the people taking part in it, but also pleases the local spirits or local deities by purifying any kind of impurity or pollution in the environment. By contrast, *sur*, the burnt offering, is very rarely done in the morning and is almost invariably done in the evening, and has the particular benefits and functions explained above.

There is another similar practice that is called the water torma, and this is almost invariably done in the early morning. Typically it consists of a type of Dzambhala practice, and then the offering of water to Dzambhala, and by doing so receiving the common and supreme attainments. In fact, the practice of water torma contains a complete practice of upward offering to the Three Jewels and downward generosity to all manner of sentient beings. I am mentioning these practices here because the practices of *sang*, *sur*, and water torma are all very easy to do and have great benefit.

Among these three types of practice, the *sur*, the burnt offering, is particularly beneficial for beings in the bardo, the period of time after death. All beings that are born will definitely at some point die, and having died will pass through the bardo. When you are in the bardo, it is said you have complete senses and the capacity to wander about without impediment. Thus for the roughly forty-nine-day period of the bardo, you have a physical existence that is similar to that of a preta, and you are only nourished by smells—for example, the smells of things that are burnt. Because of that, the most beneficial thing for those beings that have recently passed away and are in the bardo is to perform the *sur* offering. At best it should be done every day of the forty-nine-day period of someone's time in the bardo or, at least, from time to time during that period. This practice will help alleviate their suffering from hunger and thirst. This practice will be of great benefit to particular beings to whom it is dedicated, and indeed to all beings who are in the bardo at that time.

Now, all of these practices are aspects of the practice of generosity, which means that they are ways of training your mind in the practice of generosity. If you do not train your mind in generosity—if you do not consciously cultivate it—then you will be increasingly afflicted by an inability to give away or even use what you have. Whatever few possessions you have, you will be unable to give them up, and you will hold onto them with an obsessive greed, which can become so intense that you will not even dare to use them yourself. You will be obsessed with what you do not have, and you will constantly say to yourself and perhaps to others, "I do not have any food; I do not have any clothes; I do not have any money; I do not have this, I do not have that." You will be unable to use what you do have in offerings to the Three Jewels, in generosity to other beings, or even to make practical use of these things for your own benefit. In short, if you do not cultivate generosity, while you will continue for some time to have a human body, you will have the mind of a preta.

For example, I remember that in the news some time ago there was a story about an elderly woman who was often seen in the subways of New York City during the winter. She was rarely there during the summer, but during the winter she would be seen begging in the subway stations. After some years of this, she died while begging in the subway. When they looked at her belongings and found out her address, it turned out she was from New Mexico. She owned a house there and had fifty thousand dollars in the bank. She was unable to make use of her own money and her own possessions, but for some reason felt compelled to stay in a freezing subway station in New York City and eventually she died there. The point is that if you have resources, at least you should use them to take care of yourself — that is perfectly alright — but to have such resources and not make use of them and then die in misery is pointless.

Then going beyond that, whatever you have, you should make offerings to the Three Jewels and to the needy. This is extremely important. It is so important that it was said by Jetsun Milarepa to always practice generosity even if you have to take food out of your own mouth in order to do so.

If you cannot conquer obsessive selfishness, then even if you came to control all of the wealth in this entire world of Jambudvipa, you would be unsatisfied. Lacking contentment, you would think, "Well, there must be other planets that I could get the money from as well." Another situation is where you think, "Well, I can not give up any of my own possessions. I need what I have now, so maybe I'll make some extra money that I can use to make offerings to the Three Jewels or perform generosity." In that way you postpone acts of generosity endlessly.

Material generosity, the first of the three types of generosity, was primarily taught with practitioners who are householders in mind. Householders are people who have families and homes, and are using their domestic and general life situations to train in the bodhicittas of aspiration and implementation and to cultivate the six perfections. If you are not a householder, meaning that you are an ordained monk or nun, then the lifestyle that is prescribed is to cultivate contentment and austerity in all situations. This means to survive on barely enough, to have a minimum of food and clothing and a very austere dwelling in solitude and so

116

on, and to use that type of extremely simplified living situation in order to one-pointedly cultivate the three trainings of *shila* (discipline), *samadhi* (meditation), and *prajna* (knowledge).

The distinction being made here is that an ordained person, one who is living in an austere way in order to practice Dharma fully, should not abandon the austerity of their living situation and the amount of time they spend in practice in order to accumulate wealth that they can thereby use to practice generosity. They should not use the practice of generosity as an excuse to focus less on their training. Thus for such a person, it is of the utmost importance, in all ways and all situations, to cultivate contentment.

The second type of material generosity is called great giving. Great giving refers to the giving of material things that are very precious or very rare, such as your most precious possessions. This is explained in terms of giving things that would be very valuable in traditional societies, such as domestic animals, and relinquishing attachment to members of your family, giving precious jewels or extremely precious or costly things, and so forth.

The third category of material generosity is called utmost generosity, and this is something that cannot usually be practiced by ordinary beings. It can only really be done by those who have attained the bodhisattva levels (*bhumis*). It means to give up your body or parts of your body, such as your limbs and even your life, for the benefit of others. There are well-known examples of this, such as when the Buddha in a previous life was born as the king named Great Courage, and fed his own body to a starving tigress. This took place in the region of Nepal that is now known as Namo Buddha. There are other examples, such as when the great Buddhist teacher Arya Nagarjuna offered his very head to someone. This is what is called the utmost generosity. It should be made clear that other than those who have attained the bodhisattva levels, ordinary beings cannot actually implement this type of generosity. What we can do is aspire to do it in the future by mentally dedicating our lives, our bodies, and so forth, to the benefit of other beings.

The second major category of generosity is dharmic generosity or the giving of Dharma. This means to bestow empowerments, transmissions, and instructions on others, and in general to encourage others in appropriate ways to acts of virtue. The most important thing when you are practicing the generosity of the Dharma is that your motivation be correct. This means you should never teach with the attitude, "Well, I'm teaching these people so I can become famous or prosperous." You should always do it with the attitude that you are trying to teach people what will actually benefit them most, with the motivation to benefit them, and in appropriate ways that they can make use of.

The third category of generosity is the generosity of protection. This means protecting beings that need it under specific circumstances. In particular it means protecting beings from serious harm. It can also mean befriending those who lack supportive relationships, and so forth. In this category is the saving of lives, which was taught by the Buddha to be the most beneficial type of material virtue. This means that as much as you can, you should save lives, especially animals that would otherwise be killed. For example, if you have the power and influence to do so, it means to protect the lives of animals on a certain mountain or certain valley, or to save the lives or ransom the lives of other animals that would definitely be killed. One example of this that is easy to practice these days is to buy and release small animals such as worms and small fish that are being sold as bait for fishermen. If these are released harmlessly into a natural setting, there is actually a double karmic benefit. Not only are the animals saved from a painful death, but also fewer fish may be caught, saving them as well.

I would like to mention that the practice of generosity is essential in the practice of vajrayana, which indeed must always take place within the mahayana outlook. In fact, generosity is one of the root commitments (samayas) of the

118

vajrayana. When you take the vajrayana samayas of the five families — in particular when you take the samayas of the ratna or jewel family — you say, "I will continually cultivate the four generosities." The four generosities are the three generosities that were just mentioned and the generosity of loving-kindness.

The second of the six perfections is morality. This also has three aspects: the morality of abstention from evil, the morality of the implementation of virtue, and the morality of benefiting beings. The first of these is the morality which is abstention from evil or wrongdoing, and this means to rigorously abstain from any kind of wrongdoing with body, speech, and mind, activities that are of no help to others and only bring them harm. The general categorization of wrongdoing as the ten unvirtuous actions of body, speech, and mind, was mentioned in the opening section of the book. Since detailed explanations of this topic are often given in Buddhist teachings and texts, it is not necessary to do that here.

The second type of morality is the morality of the implementation of virtue, which means accumulating virtuous actions. This means to engage in all kinds of virtue and never to neglect a virtuous action because it seems too insignificant. The reason that it is necessary for us to be so painstaking in our implementation of virtuous actions — even ones that seem insignificant or too small — is that, as is said, we must cultivate virtue intentionally with all of our faculties, such as our speech and so on, because we are automatically accumulating negative actions all the time merely by walking around. This means that we cannot help but do unvirtuous things simply through being alive. As human beings, we are not the biggest sentient being there is, but from the point of view of an insect we are very big. Every time you walk, you step on insects and kill them, and every time you sit down we are killing things. Therefore, minor acts of virtue such as reciting mantras like *om mani peme hung,* turning prayer wheels, and so on, help to intentionally counteract the types of negative actions that we are

119

doing unconsciously all the time. In short, it is necessary to maintain mindfulness and alertness as much as you can and be careful in all of your actions. We must be careful to avoid that which is harmful to others and to adopt that which is helpful, because if you are careless, then even in an attempt to play or joke around, you can actually accumulate a serious amount of negativity.

The idea that we are constantly (and usually unknowingly) killing beings was taught by the Buddha. Although this notion is present in the Buddha's teachings, we do not need to merely rely on the Buddha's statements about it. It can be seen clearly from a scientific viewpoint as well. We know that every time we wash our hands or every time we take medicine for a minor ailment, we are killing lots of bacteria. Since we cannot live without killing or seriously harming sentient beings, we need to counteract this through the practice of virtue.

We should never think that a small act of wrongdoing is harmless. A small negative act can bring ruin, just as one spark can burn down a huge haystack. On the other hand, a small act of virtue can bring great benefit, so if you constantly maintain mindfulness and alertness, you will constantly find opportunities to perform acts of virtue that will bring about a great accumulation of virtue. For example, when you are walking along a road or path, you can always move insects out of the path where they would be killed. In such ways we have constant opportunities to save lives.

With all this in mind, you should not look down on even small virtuous actions. Remember that even small drops of water will eventually fill a huge pot, and if you continually practice these small virtuous actions, you can eventually accumulate vast amounts of merit. Small virtuous actions, even if unintentional, accumulate merit. For example, there is a story that at one time a pig was walking along a road, and on the side of the road was a stupa. The pig, of course, had no intention whatsoever of circumambulating that stupa, but walking along the same road was a dog, which also had no intention of circumambulating the stupa. When the dog saw the pig, the dog started chasing the pig. In running around, they both ended up circumambulating the stupa. It is said that they both accumulated vast amounts of merit from that.

Since there are constant opportunities to accumulate wrongdoing and virtue, we must therefore always keep in mind the importance of abandoning even the smallest wrongdoing and practicing even the smallest virtue. As well, we must dedicate the merit of doing both to the awakening of all beings.

The third aspect of morality is the morality of benefiting beings, which refers to the motivation behind what we do. Essentially it is the morality of constantly maintaining the altruistic motivation of doing whatever you do for the benefit of others and not for your own profit. For beginners, the most important thing in connection with morality is to practice as much virtue as you can, to abandon as much wrongdoing as you can, and to dedicate the virtue of it to the spiritual awakening of all beings without exception.

Why is it taught that the most important thing for beginners to practice is the practice of virtue, and the dedication of that virtue to all beings? The reason is that in order to be of actual direct benefit to beings in the specific sense of liberating them or teaching Dharma to them, you need to really have the ability to do so. The ability to do that is something more than just being able to communicate the Dharma based on your own understanding — an understanding that could, in fact, be quite uncertain. To be able to benefit beings by teaching Dharma and guiding them toward liberation in that way requires that you have such stability that your own qualities and understanding are like an inexhaustible treasury. If your understanding is uncertain, then your communication of Dharma to others will have the effect of pouring out the contents of the vase of your own understanding into the vase of other beings' minds, and you will be left empty and hollow. If your understanding is really stable, then it is like an inexhaustible treasury. No matter how much Dharma you pour out to others, you will never become empty, you will be unaffected, and your qualities will be undiminished.

In the practice of virtue it is also of the utmost importance to combine all virtuous actions with what are called "the three excellences." The first is excellence in the beginning, which is the proper motivation. This is established by going for refuge and generating bodhicitta at the beginning of the practice session. The second is the excellence of nonconceptuality during the practice itself, which refers to engaging in the main practice, whatever it may be, without distractions and conceptuality, and the third is the excellence of dedication, which refers to the dedication and aspiration for the enlightenment of all beings at the end of the session.

The third of the six perfections is patience, which also has three varieties. The first is patience or forbearance with the abuse of others, the second is patience with the austerities of Dharma practice, and the third is patience or tolerance for the inconceivably profound meaning.

The first of these three kinds of patience refers to how you deal with a situation where you are being harmed by someone. This harm could be done directly to you, or more indirectly—i.e., behind your back. The direct harm is a situation where someone physically hurts you, verbally abuses you, steals your possessions, or destroys something that belongs to you. The abuse of harming you behind your back would be, for example, when someone says that you said something you did not say, or that you did something you did not do, and so on. In either case, the practice of patience with the abuse is not to become angry at the person, but to generate loving-kindness and compassion for them, and to try your best to help them.

In the particular situation we each find ourselves in, whether it is relating to family members, engaging in our professional or work life, or living together and working at a Dharma center in close community, we obviously have an excellent opportunity for practicing this first type of patience. As is said, if there is nothing that could make you angry, how could you cultivate patience? Since we have lots of situations in which we would tend otherwise to become angry, we have lots of situations in which we can cultivate the perfection of patience.

Especially, we need to acknowledge that we all have a complete set of the five root kleshas (mental afflictions). As ordinary beings, none of us has attained buddhahood. Therefore there are constant conflicts. At the same time, while we all have a complete set of the kleshas (which are also called the five poisons), everyone's set is slightly different. Thus we have different proportions of these patterns. Some people have tremendous pride, other people have tremendous anger, and so on. It would be perhaps even more difficult if we all had the same proportions of these negative qualities—if we all, for example, had tremendous anger. However, we are all a little bit different, so the situation can be worked on.

To take an example, let's say that there was one person in the community who had a real problem with anger—who was constantly getting angry for very little reason. If nobody understood that pattern, then when that person got angry at us, we would be horribly shocked and unsettled by it. However, if as a community we understood that this person had a tremendous problem with anger, then we would in fact be prepared to deal with the situation. As well, when you know beforehand that this person has such a problem with anger, then when they get angry, you would be prepared for that. At that point your reaction really depends upon you. If you are a practitioner, then when he or she comes under the power of anger once again, you have the opportunity to recognize the fact that you have a great opportunity to apply the appropriate remedy to the situation.

When someone becomes angry with you, if you respond with anger, then it is like pouring oil on a fire. His or her anger will grow and the situation will get worse. If you respond with patience — which does not mean that you will not feel angry, because of course you have the klesha of anger yourself — it means that you will not allow yourself to be controlled by your anger. If you respond with that kind of patience, then the other person's anger will tend to fall flat, because their anger is like a drumstick that they are holding up like a club. They need a drum to beat it on in order to make a noise. If you do not give them the drum by not falling under the power of your own anger, then they can not really make that much of a noise. This means that you will benefit yourself greatly through strengthening the habit of patience, and you also benefit the other person by allowing for the pacification of their anger.

Living in the world, with work, family, and community involvements, we have a tremendous and constant opportunity to practice this discipline of patience. If you *can* practice it, if you can avoid returning anger toward others when they are angry with you, then you can accumulate vast amounts of merit simply by doing that. As is said in the *Bodhicharyavatara*, all of the merit of generosity and of offerings to the buddhas that have been performed over one hundred eons is destroyed in one instant of strong anger. Therefore since anger is the greatest of evils, then patience is the greatest of virtues. As is said, "As there is no evil like anger, there is no virtuous austerity like patience, so therefore seek to cultivate patience in all ways and all situations." Understanding this, we will see the importance of continually keeping the defects of anger in mind, as well as the benefits of patience, and of trying to cultivate patience in all difficult situations.

It is said that there is no wrongdoing like anger, and there is no virtue like patience. The point of this is that while anger is the worst of the kleshas, it is something that is part of our makeup, and therefore it is the case that we are going to continue to get angry, so the practice of patience requires some effort. Therefore it is an act of virtue—or we could say it is austerity because it is non-indulgence. Therefore if you can maintain patience, even in situations that would normally make you very angry, then you are cultivating one of the greatest virtues that there is. You should do this using any method you can.

It was said by Padampa Sangye, "The experience of others as enemies is a confused projection, so relinquish spite towards your enemies, people of Ding Ri." (Ding Ri is a place in Tibet, and this is one of a number of Dharma sayings that Padampa Sangye gave to the people there by way of advice.) In a similar vein, Atisha said, "Do not get angry at those who harm you. If you get angry at those who harm you, then when will you find the opportunity to practice patience?"

Therefore when people abuse you verbally or physically, or make false accusations about your behavior and so on, neither react on the spot with fury nor hold a grudge. If you can stop reacting immediately and holding grudges, then you have found a way to remove a great deal of your previous wrongdoing and obscurations.

If you can cultivate patience continually, so that you are not overpowered by your anger, then you will accumulate vast amounts of merit. At best, you should see those who harm you as your guru, in which case, by reflecting upon the fact that they are the supreme basis for your cultivation of loving-kindness, compassion, and patience, you will understand that they are like your teachers or gurus. This is the best attitude to take, but it is very difficult. If you cannot take precisely that attitude, then at least you should try to be able to reflect that such aggression from others is a necessary condition for your practice of patience, and have that degree of gratitude.

From the way we think about people and speak about them, it is clear that anger is really the greatest fault. For example, we might speak of someone we know and say, "Well, he's really very bright, and he's certainly very diligent in practice, but he gets angry all the time," and that implies that we just cannot deal with him. From seeing how we react to people who are angry, it is clear that anger is the most serious defect — the most devastating klesha — of the mind. The fact is that you cannot really be a good person and be angry all the time. It was said by Padampa Sangye that, "One hundred karmas accumulated through desire do not equal one negative karma accumulated through anger."

For this reason, it is taught that people who are really trying to practice Dharma properly need to be as gentle and fluffy as soft cotton in their conduct of body, speech, and mind. This image is used because no matter how you handle or touch unspun cotton, it always feels soft. A practitioner needs to be like that, in the sense that no matter what the situation is, he or she is always gentle. If you do even a little bit of practice and maintain a little bit of inner commitment to this — and are without arrogance about it — then even by doing that much, you can pacify your body, speech, and mind and make them gentle. The point of doing practice is to be able to tame ourselves in this way.

If this is not what happens, if practice does not tame your body, speech, and mind, then even if you have some qualities, such as having some knowledge of Dharma or having done a certain amount of practice, you will have tremendous arrogance about it. You will constantly be thinking, "Well, I have meditated upon such and such deities; I have recited so many mantras and met such and such lamas, and so on," and you will be comparing yourself to others. You will think, "Well, they do not do these practices, they do not know this much about Dharma, they have not met such and such lamas," and so on. This arrogance will make your mind so tight that when someone says one word to you that seems to be some kind of difference of opinion, you will immediately explode in anger, because you are completely paranoiac. Everything everyone says will seem like some kind of put down or subtle criticism. In short you will always be ready to blow up; you will always be on the brink of anger. If you become like this even though you are practicing Dharma, it means that the Dharma and your mind have from the very beginning been completely unconnected, and that none of the practice you have done has accomplished the slightest benefit whatsoever for you. It was said by Geshe Chengawa, "When people practice hearing, reflection, and meditation upon the Buddhadharma, and yet while they are doing so, their obsession with their imputed self grows stronger and stronger, their patience diminishes to the size of a pea, and they become more irritable than trolls—this indicates that their practice is in some way faulty."

Geshe Chengawa continues by saying, "Rather than that, always keep low," which means always maintain a low position to prevent the development of arrogance or pride. The quote continues, " . . .wear rags . . ." This does not literally mean that you should always wear rags; it means that you should not be attached to clothing and should regard clothing as functional. It goes on, "Place all above you, good, bad, or in between." This does not mean that you should literally treat everyone the way you would treat your teachers. It means that you should not compare yourself with others and should respect everyone without trying to divide people into those you think are better than you and those you think are worse than you. He concludes, "But keep love, compassion, and bodhicitta as the essence of your Dharma. Rather than running after profound views and high words, taking patience as the essence of your practice will be more effective."

The second type of patience is having patience with the austerities involved in Dharma practice. The basic idea is that in order to practice effectively, you have to accept the hardships that practice will entail, the experience of heat and cold, hunger and thirst, and so on. As an example of this, it is said in the tantras that we should be willing to cross ravines of "fire and razors" in order to find the Dharma.

There is a quote from Jetsun Milarepa that expresses the wish to have this kind of patience. He said:

> To be without people asking after my health if I'm ill
> And to die without people coming to view my body,
> And to die in this place of retreat
> If I can accomplish these things
> Then the wishes of this yogi will be fully
> accomplished.

> To have no footprints at my door
> And no blood left inside my cave
> And if I can die in this place of retreat
> Then the wishes of this yogi will be completely
> accomplished.

> If no one will ask where I went
> And if I have no idea where I'm going
> If I can die in this place of retreat
> The wishes of this yogi will be fully accomplished.

> If my rotting corpse is consumed by insects
> And my muscles and sinews sucked dry by flies
> And if I can die in this place of retreat
> Then the wishes of this yogi will be fully
> accomplished.

The line about having "no footprints at my door and no blood left inside my cave" means that his body will have been completely consumed by wild animals such that nothing goes to waste. The whole quotation is an expression of the best kind of patience and renunciation in relation to practice. Of course, if you are the best type of practitioner, then you can literally emulate Jetsun Milarepa's example.

It is important, however, to distinguish between a sincere natural inclination towards a fully renunciate lifestyle, and what could be called ephemeral renunciation. Ephemeral renunciation occurs when we first meet our teachers and we become tremendously inspired by what we hear and what we see, and then for a moment we forget the world entirely and we want to be just like Milarepa. We run off to a cave somewhere and we try our best in our feeble way to imitate Milarepa's mode of conduct. We might last a week or so, but by that time we are so hungry and cold that we are completely miserable. We remember the world and end up running back to it. Rather than that, it is much better to start slowly, with a gradual and regular practice. By developing your practice in that way, you can eventually come to develop a full certainty about the Dharma, at which point you will never turn back in your practice. That is the best way to emulate Jetsun Milarepa.

The third type of patience is not being afraid of the profound meaning. This means that when you hear an explanation of the nature of things — emptiness — rather than getting upset or scared about it, you learn to understand it in its proper context and relate to it. This actually can be a problem. For example, there is a story about two Indian monks who came to receive teachings from Lord Atisha. He began to explain to them the first aspect of emptiness, which is the selflessness of persons. When he explained the selflessness of persons to them, they said, "That's wonderful and very profound and thank you for explaining that." Then Atisha went on to explain the other half of emptiness which is the selflessness of things and the non-inherent existence of all phenomena. When he got to that point, they became very frightened and they actually blocked their ears. They said, "Do not say that; do not say that stuff." Atisha was somewhat disappointed by their reaction. He said later that although those two were very good monks, the problem was that, not having trained their mind in loving-kindness, compassion, and bodhicitta, they could not hear or understand the profound Dharma. That being the case, there was not much use in their merely having a monastic lifestyle. The point of not being afraid of the profound meaning means not to close your ears to the truth. Thus the third type of patience, the patience of not being afraid of emptiness, is very important.

QUESTIONS AND ANSWERS

Question: About patience — it seems that the more I develop it, the more it is tested, and the more of it I need! Am I doing something wrong here?

Rinpoche: You are not doing anything wrong — that is the natural situation. For example, when you have not in any way developed a skill, then you see no opportunities for employing that skill. When you start to develop that skill, then you start to see more and more opportunities for its employment. Therefore having your patience tested is a good thing.

It is similar to learning meditation. When you begin to do the practice, you have an experience that is very similar in some sense. When you have not done much meditation practice, you have no idea how many thoughts or kleshas there are running through your mind all the time. Then when you start to practice meditation, you actually start to recognize the presence of thoughts and kleshas. At that point it seems to you as though you are having more thoughts and more kleshas than you used to. In fact that is not the case. What is happening is that you are recognizing the ones that were already there, but it seems to you as though it is getting worse. In fact, it is not. In the same way, as you consciously begin to practice patience, more challenges can definitely come up.

Question: This question is concerning the whole issue of patience and anger, specifically in connection with a long-standing relationship in which there is a history of anger or hurt. In that situation it is very easy to get your buttons pushed, at which point there is a whole involved story and history that comes up. What are the best methods for dealing with the history, the anger itself, and for developing patience?

Rinpoche: The issue here is one of habit, a long-standing habit. The basic solution is that the momentum of Dharma can counteract the momentum of the negative habit. We all have different kinds of habits based upon the choices that we have made. Some of these are good and some of these are bad. For example, if you have a habit of getting angry, and then if today you allow yourself to be overpowered by the anger and you act it out, then tomorrow there will be that much more tendency to get angry. Thus if it has been going on for a long time, you are in a sense well along the path of disaster. The beginning of the way out of this is to recognize that you have a choice not to be that way. The anger is not your essential being. It is something that has happened to you, but it is not your basic nature. Instead, your basic nature is buddha nature—the enlightened quality we all have. Since the anger is not intrinsic to your being, you have the potential to reverse that pattern.

Habits are like something that is wound up very tight, and there is no way you can unwind it by winding it up even tighter. You have to go in the opposite direction—against the grain, so to speak. Therefore you have to start unwinding this habit. Practically speaking, this means that in any situation in which you are becoming angry and upset, you need to apply the appropriate remedy. In the case of anger, irritation, and resentment, the remedy is patience. Of course, this is very difficult. It is very easy for anyone to feel love and compassion for someone who does not upset them—for someone who is loving to them and that they love very much. On the other hand, it is very hard for anyone, no matter who they are, to feel love and compassion for an enemy. Just because it is difficult, though, does not mean it is impossible. It is a matter of going through the process of unwinding the habit until you can feel this kind of patience and compassion.

Question: You spoke about the Karmapa as being the embodiment of compassion. The Dalai Lama has also been called the buddha of compassion. Could you explain a bit about that?

Rinpoche: They are equally embodiments of the compassion of all buddhas, because they are equally emanations of the Bodhisattva Chenrezig. Thus there is no conflict in saying that His Holiness the Karmapa is the embodiment of the compassion of all buddhas, and saying His Holiness the Dalai Lama is the embodiment of the compassion of all buddhas. In liturgies of praise to Chenrezig there are statements like, "Each of your thousand arms is a chakravartin, and each of the eyes in the hands of those thousand arms is a buddha." Thus there can be many embodiments of the compassion of Chenrezig. I have focused on the Gyalwa Karmapa because our tradition is Kagyu, but we could easily say the same things about the Dalai Lama.

Question: Is there a remedy that can help prevent me from falling into idiot generosity? By that I mean trying to be very nice all the time, and letting people draw me into their projects. It seems like I end up very busy, and people are basically taking advantage of me. Is there a way to counteract this?

Rinpoche: The only remedy for this is to use your own intelligence and to make your choices consciously. However, there are two situations which are quite different in nature and which may appear similar. The first is where you are in fact being taken advantage of, harmed, or deceived by others. In that case, the remedy is to use your own intelligence, because there is no standard formula for knowing when people are going to deceive you.

The other situation, which may look similar in certain respects but is fundamentally different, is where it is really *you* who are being deceptive. In that case it may be that you are pretending to be extremely selfless and compassionate and generous — and acting in that way — in order to satisfy some sort of hidden need or achieve some kind of hidden ambition that you have. This may be something that you are not even consciously aware of. In that kind of situation, you are actually being the deceptive person.

In the beginning, you may not know how to judge situations. In order to cultivate and sharpen the intelligence needed to judge or to choose more accurately, you can study the teachings of the Buddha. The Dharma contains a great deal of very practical advice about such matters. If you really come to understand this, you will have a good idea of how to make such choices.

Question: What are the main methods for developing patience?

Rinpoche: The primary method is meditation on compassion. The key to the development of compassion, which produces patience, seems to be to begin with using someone for whom it is easy to feel compassion. That way you get the feeling for compassion. Then you expand it from that into what is called a neutral object (in other words, a being for whom you do not have strong feelings either way), and then you progress to very difficult objects. Traditionally it is taught that you start by generating compassion for the person or persons you love most. This could be your parents, although in today's world it is not always certain that people are on good terms with their parents. In any case you would start with anyone you actually love most, and then you extend from them into more difficult beings, and that is how it's developed.

In using this method of starting with someone we love, we have to be very careful, because there is a difference between loving-kindness in the sense of wishing beings to be happy, and being personally attached to someone. When we are attached to someone, they can seem very close, and the kind of involvement that is based on attachment is often what we mean when we use the word "love". This type of love is very different in nature from the type of love that is based on altruistic concern. In the type of love that is based upon attachment, you may have thoughts like, "Oh, I would die for you," and so on. This seems very altruistic, but it is

133

all fundamentally based upon attachment to that person as a part of your world.

The love that is based on attachment is not really love at all, because it is fundamentally self-serving. The sign of this is that as long as that person or those persons serve the function that you want them to have in your world, as long as they do for you what you want, then you seem to love them so much. Then as soon as they stop being what you want them to be, the love vanishes. This means it was not love at all, it was attachment. What we mean by actual love here is a concern for the welfare of other beings that is completely devoid of any kind of payback personally, and that has nothing whatsoever to do with hoping that that person will act a certain way toward you and fearing that they will not.

Question: It seems to me that patience is sometimes seen as a weakness, and it just becomes an opportunity for one person to abuse another.

Rinpoche: This brings up the fact that the cultivation of love or benevolence has to be combined with the use of prajna or intelligence, because in fact a love that is divorced from intelligence will not be successful. You need the combination of both. This intelligent love will not make you a pushover. It will not make you a willing victim. This applies both to individuals or groups of people. Intelligent love looks to see what is actually going to be beneficial in a situation, and will not take simplistic attitudes like, "Now that I've cultivated love, anyone can do whatever they want to me, people can walk all over me," and so on. Because you know when you look at the situation, if you see that allowing someone to abuse you will do them no good, it will do you no good, will not do any third party any good, then you will not allow the abuse to continue. But this means that in your remedy or in your dealing with the abuse, while you will not allow the person to harm you or control you, you will not seek revenge. You may have to put a stop to the situation, which might mean escaping by running away, but you would not attempt to use the situation as an excuse for destroying the other person.

Question: Say there is a person you know who is angry all the time, and it seems that they mainly want you to agree with them about certain things. Clearly if you agree with them, there is a kind of calming effect. But then you are left with whatever you have agreed with, which will come up again in a negative way, because maybe you actually had a different opinion. Maybe you really do not agree. But saying that in the first place would be inflaming them and fueling their anger. What is the proper thing to do?

Rinpoche: It depends on the importance of the situation and what the effects will be of agreeing or appearing to agree or disagree with the person. In general, while we need to practice the six perfections, we also need to fit in the world, and we have to therefore be very careful and skillful in how we apply all of this. When the person you have to deal with always has to be agreed with or they will get angry, if it is important that you convey your opinion, then you have to look very carefully at the situation and see, for example, how is he today? What do you think will happen if you dare to disagree with this person on this particular day? Do you think they will be able to hear it? If you believe that if you say something in the right way, such that you are not confrontational with them—meaning that you do not present yourself in opposition to them but you are just giving your own view—if you think that they might be able to hear it, then you should say something. But if you see that they are already so angry that anything you say is just going to make them angrier, then you should probably wait.

Question: I have a question about people who do not practice the Dharma. If by walking and sitting down and just being alive they kill many beings, and they have no way of counteracting this through virtuous activity—nor do they know about the dedication of merit, so the possibility is that by one rage of anger they can destroy any virtue they *have* accumulated—is it true that they are then very close to going to the lower realms? There are so many people like this in this time we are in.

Rinpoche: Well, not only people such as that, but also we ourselves are in very great danger of going to the lower realms. This is not a one-time thing—it is a continual process. The point is that we have been reborn so many times and over such a long period of time that we have a vast variety of karmic imprints within us. We have immeasurable amounts of virtuous karma and immeasurable amounts of unvirtuous karma. Generally speaking, the strongest karmic imprint is the one that will ripen first. Therefore, it is not always certain that what you have done in this life is necessarily going to be the primary factor in the type of existence you assume in the next life. Therefore I could not guarantee one hundred percent that even someone who is leading a miserable existence which consists entirely of indulgence of their kleshas is going to be reborn in the lower realms such as the hell realms. That is because I do not know what they were doing in past lives, and they may have a stronger virtuous karma that would manifest first.

It is very difficult for us to understand the workings of karma directly. We can understand the general principles, but we do not know all of the factors when it comes to specifics. Someone like the Buddha, who can see everything in the universe in the past, present, and future at one time, like something placed in the palm of his hand, can directly see the causes and results of actions. The Buddha can see what they are doing now and what births this will lead to in the future, but it is very difficult for us to know this.

Question: When you spoke about cultivating contentment that was the first time I think I have heard contentment spoken of that way. I always thought contentment was an outcome of the way things were, or the way we would like them to be. I am just trying to understand what it would mean to *cultivate* contentment. Would that be part of patience, or part of practicing the six paramitas altogether?

136

Rinpoche: Actually, contentment and patience are somewhat different in the way we are using them here. The mention of contentment I made was in the context of a very specific context, namely the attitude of an ordained monk or nun. Of course, everyone needs contentment to some degree, but what was being talked about there was the contentment or the degree of contentment that is appropriate for a renunciate — a man or woman who has taken vows of celibacy. Such a person, because of their lifestyle, has no mundane or secular responsibilities beyond his or her own physical survival. By contrast, a householder — someone with a family — is responsible to take care of their family. Therefore they have to work, and they cannot be content with just their own physical survival. They have to really move beyond that, and they have to actually make career plans, make a good living, and so on.

Because ordained monks or nuns have no responsibilities that justify that degree of involvement, it is taught that they should not allow themselves to become what we would call a career person in the world. They should be content with mere physical survival. If celibates get involved with a worldly ambition, which is unnecessary for them because of their lifestyle, then they are losing their opportunity and freedom to practice, which is the entire point of their ordination. On the other hand, if a householder is too content with their own physical survival and thinks, "Well, my belly's full, I do not have to worry about anything else; my family can starve and that's OK," then they're not fulfilling their responsibilities either.

Question: When you spoke about the perfection of generosity, I was not quite clear on what makes generosity perfect.

Rinpoche: The basic meaning of the word "perfection" here is that it represents the full completion or consummation of a specific virtue. Using generosity as an example, when we are journeying on the path, the virtue that we use to progress is generosity. On the basis of practicing or cultivating generosity, the generosity itself and the qualities that come about from the practice of generosity gradually become developed until they reach their full measure, or are perfected, at which point it becomes the perfection of generosity.

Question: I did not really understand what you meant by saying the generosity was "sealed" with something non-conceptual.

Rinpoche: That refers to perfect or pure generosity, which is the result of the practice of generosity. At this point whenever we perform an act of generosity, we do so with a conceptualization of the elements of the act. For example we think, "I am giving this to him." Ultimate or pure generosity, the true perfection of generosity, is when there is no conceptualization of the truly existent giver, gift, or recipient. That is the result of a long training in generosity. It is at that point that generosity comes to be "sealed" by the view of profound emptiness.

In the present situation, since our practice of virtues such as generosity still includes a conceptualization of the elements of the action, then although we are attempting to follow the example of all buddhas and bodhisattvas of the past in their cultivation of the six perfections, we need to be careful how we do it. Given that we are still afflicted by conceptualization, if we give something that is too big for us to handle giving, then we may regret it afterwards and experience attachment, which is a problem. Thus we should always make sure that our practice of generosity is not going to cause us regret, based on greed or attachment. When you get to the point where there is no longer any conceptualization of the giver, the gift, and the recipient, and then all thoughts of greed—and indeed thoughts of ownership—are gone and there will be no regret, which is the ultimate practice and final result of generosity. This applies to other kinds of virtues as well.

It is very important that your offerings be made without greed or regret. If you think when you are giving something that, "Well, I've lost so much in doing this," then it is actually not virtue. It is a wrongdoing. For example, even if the most you offer is one lamp filled with oil, and then if you can offer it without a regret, that is pure virtue. On the other hand, if in offering it you think, "Well, I've used up one lamp's worth of oil on this nonsense," then it will do you more harm than good. It would be better not to do it at all.

Question: In thinking about giving, I notice that in myself I do not have a completely single-minded point of view about it. There are lots of sides to me. From one side I might feel very generous, and then something else bubbles up at another time that might be contradictory and I need to work it out. Isn't that just part of the human condition? If I were to wait until I was a hundred percent all on line for something, I might never do anything positive.

Rinpoche: This is an example of why all of the virtuous actions we as ordinary beings perform are called "defiled virtue" at this point, because nothing is ever quite perfect in terms of our attitude. At the same time, though we call it defiled virtue, it is still very helpful. If we were to classify it as good or bad, it is definitely good – certainly it is not bad, but it is not as good as undefiled virtue. Because of the importance of developing undefiled virtue, we discuss what virtues such as generosity are like in their purest form. In that context we say that generosity has to be without any attachment or regret whatsoever. As you say, we cannot guarantee it will always be like that. We just have to do our best, and try to be as close to perfect as we can be in our practice of generosity. Where you can draw the line, for example, in an act of generosity or an act of offering or whatever, is if you perform the generosity and you feel a little bit of regret, a little bit of hesitation or a little bit of greed, then that is really OK. Having performed the act of generosity and regretting it a little bit is better than not having performed it at all. On the other hand, if you perform an act of generosity and you regret it tremendously, and you are ferociously attached to what you gave up and you intensely wish you had not given it away, in that case it would be better not to have done it.

(END OF QUESTIONS AND ANSWERS)

The fourth perfection is diligence, and it has three aspects, which are the diligence that is like armor, the diligence of application, and what is known as "the diligence that is never content."

The first of the three types of diligence is armorlike diligence. Essentially this means not being timid with regard to the austerities of practice. When you reflect on the lives of the great teachers and buddhas and bodhisattvas of the past, and you reflect upon their austerities and their deeds, you may have doubts that you can follow their example. You may think, "Well, they are buddhas and bodhisattvas after all, and so of course they can do those things; ordinary people like myself could not possibly follow their example." This type of timidity is not appropriate. You should rather think that it is through those deeds and those austerities that those teachers attained their siddhi or attainment. Since we are following their example, it is the case that we must follow their example in all ways. Perhaps we cannot do better than they did, but at least we should try our best to apply the same diligence. Furthermore, if they were bodhisattvas and needed to engage in such austerities in order to attain awakening, how much more must we, who are ordinary beings, need to do so? In short, an attitude of courage towards these austerities and great deeds is the diligence that is like armor.

Therefore the attitude that expresses this armorlike diligence would be, "Well, I do not have much of a natural residue of training from previous lives, so therefore I must work very, very hard and must engage in all manner of great deeds and austerities." As well, we should take the attitude, "At this time in which I have acquired the precious human existence, with its freedoms and resources, have met quali-

fied teachers and have received the most profound instructions of all Dharma, how could I not make use of it with the
utmost diligence?" That kind of stable, courageous commitment is also an aspect of armorlike diligence.

The second type of diligence is the diligence of application,
which means that you immediately apply this commitment
to practice rather than procrastinating. It is very easy for us
to have the wish — perhaps an intense wish — to practice, but
to think that the conditions are not right and therefore say,
"I will practice tomorrow" or "I will practice next year."
But if you maintain an attitude of procrastination, then day
by day your life will be used up. Therefore do not spend
your life wishing to practice, but actually apply it. It was
said by the Drupchen Pema Karpo that a human life is really like the situation of an animal that is about to be butch-
ered. In every moment we get closer and closer to our deaths,
so to think we will practice later today or tomorrow will
cause us one day to end up lying on our deathbed knowing
that we are about to die without ever having practiced.
Therefore you should practice as soon as you have the opportunity to do so.

In short, you should never allow your wish to practice to be
corrupted by the habit of procrastination. How should you
relate to practice? Traditionally it is said that you should
relate to it with the urgency of a young man into whose lap
a snake has just fallen, or a beautiful woman who notices
that her hair has suddenly caught on fire.

If you do not take this attitude of urgency or priority, then
your mundane responsibilities, which are your primary
concern at this time, will never be finished. There will never
come a time where you will have fulfilled all of your responsibilities, because one mundane involvement produces
another, like waves on the surface of water. Thus if you keep
on waiting for your responsibilities to be completely fulfilled, there will never come a time for you to practice. The
only way to complete your responsibilities is to cast them
aside decisively.

About this, the omniscient Longchenpa said, "Ordinarily the only time you will ever finish with mundane endeavors is at the moment of your death, but you can be finished with them by abandoning them. All of these things we do, and that we are so busy with, are really like the games of children. Therefore, when you generate the wish to practice, then rather than allowing yourself to be carried away by procrastination, exhort yourself with the recollection of impermanence, and never defer practice for any future time." That type of immediate application of the wish to practice is the diligence of application.

The third type of diligence is the diligence of never being satisfied or never being content with your degree of virtue. This means never to rest on your laurels. It means never to think, "I've done this much retreat, meditated on these deities, or done this much recitation, and that is enough; I do not need to do any more." Rather, the diligence of never being satisfied is to take the attitude that you will practice as vigorously as possible until the day of your death. It means to take the attitude that you will use this life in order to attain full awakening in this life and this body, and that you will practice without fluctuation, strongly and constantly, like the current of a river, day and night, until you attain buddhahood. The traditional example for this kind of diligence is that it is like the way a hungry yak goes about eating grass. At the moment that the yak is munching on one mouthful of grass, he is already looking to see where the next one will come from. In the same way, when you are doing practice, you should not have the attitude, "When I finish this practice that is enough, I will not have to do anymore of this." Instead you think, "When I'm done with this, I will begin the next one," and so on, so that there is an attitude that goes throughout your life of never allowing your body, speech, and mind to rest, but applying them constantly in a gradually increasing and intensifying diligence.

It was said by the Vidyadhara Dujum Lingpa, "If your diligence in practice increases as you come closer and closer to death, this is a sign that you are a practitioner who has not been spoiled by the frost." The image of "spoiled by the frost" is taken from farming. Sometimes a farmer will have some very good crops that are growing up but then they are killed by a frost. In the same way, it is possible that a practitioner might be very diligent in the beginning, but then gradually their diligence would wear down and they would burn out. What he is pointing out here is that a good practitioner will not do this but will become more and more diligent as time goes on.

This situation, which in the previous quotation was called a "practitioner killed by the frost," is something we need to watch out for. It is a particular type of defect that can occur. Sometimes in our initial involvement with practice we begin in a situation that is basically an ideal opportunity for practice, where we have almost unlimited access to many great teachers. As time goes on, we become somewhat spoiled or jaded by this. We start to take Dharma for granted, and the result of this jadedness is that we become impervious to the Dharma, at which point we are impervious to the benefit of the Dharma, of any teacher or any teaching. This is a real problem that actually can and does occur. Instead of letting this happen, we should take the attitude that until we attain full buddhahood, we still obviously have karma and habitual patterns to purify. We still need to develop the qualities of the various levels of the path and so forth. Therefore there is no reason to stop practicing. We should not have the attitude that, "Well, I'll practice when it is convenient and I will not practice when it is not convenient, and maybe I will start again later if and when it becomes convenient again." Instead, we should practice continually. This type of continual attitude — of never being satisfied with however much practice you have done — is the third type of diligence, the diligence of never being satisfied with your degree of virtue.

143

The fifth of the six perfections is the perfection of dhyana, or meditative stability. Among the six perfections this is perhaps the one we normally speak about the most. The first thing to understand about meditative stability is that it cannot be developed in any true way in the midst of distractions and disturbance. It is necessary that there be an external isolation or solitude of body which can produce an internal isolation or solitude of mind. Therefore, the first step in cultivating meditative stability is to protect yourself from distractions and disturbances of all kinds.

It was said by the Tibetan master Repa Shiwa Ö, "Being alone is the basis for buddhahood. Having one companion in accordance with the Dharma is a support for the cultivation of virtue. Having three or four or more is a cause of nothing other than attachment and aversion. Therefore, I remain alone." The point here is that attachment and desire are the greatest sources of impediments to the development of fundamental meditative stability (shamata). As long as you are not content with whatever you have, as long as you wish for more than you have, and as long as you are afflicted by this, your mind cannot rest. Furthermore, the more you have, the more you want.

Therefore, in order to develop shamata, you need to have contentment that is free of greed. It was said by Arya Nagarjuna that wealth is the cause of all disturbance, because initially you have to gather it, secondly you have to protect it, and then once you have protected it, you become obsessed with increasing it. It is the characteristic of the wealthy to be avaricious and greedy. On the other hand, if you are content with whatever you have, then as long as you have sufficient food and clothing you really need nothing more.

In short, for the development of the meditative stability of shamata, isolation is necessary. Simply by going to a place of isolation or solitude, your kleshas (such as attachment and aversion) will be pacified, and it is easy in such an environment to develop all of the qualities of the path. For that reason, isolation or solitude is the absolutely necessary preliminary for the practice of meditation.

The actual practice of meditative stability has three aspects: (1) ordinary meditative stability; (2) the meditative stability of discrimination; and (3) the meditative stability of the buddhas.

The first of these three, ordinary meditation, is sometimes called "childish, goal-directed meditation." It is defined as any meditative state in which you are intentionally trying to acquire or experience the positive experiences of bliss, clarity, and non-conceptuality, and any state in which you become attached to those experiences as they arise.

The second type of meditation is called the meditation of discrimination. At this level you are free from attachment to what is literally called the "taste" or "flavor" of meditation experience itself, such as the experiences of bliss, clarity, and non-conceptuality. However, having been freed from those experiences, you are attached to the remedy — namely the experience of emptiness.

The third type of meditation, the meditation of the buddhas, is where you have not only freed yourself from fixation on experience, you have freed yourself from fixation on emptiness, and have come to rest in that great non-conceptuality which is the direct realization of dharmata.

Common to all practices of meditation is the need for correct posture. Posture is often taught through a set of instructions called the "Seven Dharmas of Vairocana." This includes such things as having the proper gaze of the eyes, which should be neither too high nor too low. The beneficial function of having the proper posture and gaze is that if the body is erect then the subtle channels of the body are straight, in which case the winds move properly and the mind will naturally be alert and at rest. Therefore when you meditate it is best if you are not lying down or leaning in one direction or another. Then, with your mind, you perform whatever technique you are employing, such as following the breath, or directing your attention to a statue of the Buddha, and so on. The basic characteristic of the perfection of meditative stability is that it is a state of mind in which there is no fixation on anything whatsoever. It is not necessary to go into more detail about it here, particularly because the in-depth instruction in shamata practice is something that is best to get in person from a qualified instructor.

The sixth perfection is the perfection of prajna or knowledge, and it has three aspects. These are: (1) the knowledge from hearing; (2) the knowledge from reflection; and (3) the knowledge arising from meditation. The first of these three types of prajna is the prajna that arises from hearing the Dharma, which means that the words and the meaning of those words are expressed by your teacher, and that you listen to this and you understand it.

The second prajna is the prajna of reflection or consideration, which is that you do not simply stop with having heard the Dharma from your teacher, but you scrutinize, consider, or question the meaning of what you have heard. You do so until you get to the point where you have revealed and resolved any misunderstandings on your part, any lack of clarity in what you have heard. At that point you do not merely know the information, but you understand it so thoroughly that when you later go into isolated retreat, you have no need whatsoever to consult anyone else.

Third is the prajna that arises from meditation. This comes about by having first eradicated a lack of knowledge or lack of understanding through hearing the Dharma and, second, having revealed the meaning of the Dharma through careful analysis or scrutiny, and then finally, applying what you have come to understand through the previous two stages in intense practice in isolated retreat. Through this intense application of what you have received in your own experience, then you gradually come to realize the nature of all things. This realization or understanding is not something that is acquired externally. It is an internal resolution, such that you have a full discernment of the nature of things — you know exactly how things are without any doubt or hesitation.

Let's look at how this prajna of meditation arises in a more detailed way. Having eradicated any kind of conceptual doubt or misunderstanding about the nature of things through hearing and reflection, then you actually practice or implement this understanding in meditation. In doing so you resolve that the nature of all external appearances (forms, sounds, smells, tastes, and tactile sensations) are appearances that arise in your experience as projections based on confusion. In other words, they are appearance without any true existence. In that sense, appearances can be described by a set of eight analogies that are traditionally used for magical illusions.

The first of these is that they are like dreams in that they appear without having any true existence. The second is that they are like magical illusions in that they arise based upon various circumstances having come together, but without actually existing as they appear to exist. The third is that they are like optical illusions in that they are the appearances of things that do not exist at all. The fourth is that they are like mirages in that while appearing, they have no substantial or true reality that corresponds to the characteristics of their mode of appearance. The fifth is that they are like echoes in that while they appear, they are not actually present either outside or inside. The sixth is that they are like a city of gandharvas in that neither the subjective nor objective aspects of the experience have true existence — neither the supporting nor the supported. The seventh is that they are like reflections in mirrors, in that they are vivid appearances without any substantial essence or nature. The eighth is that they are like magically emanated cities or dwellings, in that they can arise in an unlimited variety of modes of appearance without any of those varieties being what they truly are or having any true existence. In short, through meditation you come to recognize that all of the external appearances are without true substantiality, and that they are like these eight analogies for illusion. They are forms of which the nature is emptiness — forms that are the display of emptiness. Thus you will come to understand that all of the objects of experience are deceptive and false in that sense.

Then there is a further recognition concerning that which experiences these appearances — the mind itself. Through examining the mind's nature, you will come to recognize that the subjective aspect of experience, what we call the mind, is also without substantial existence. Thus not only will your fixated conceptualization of the inherent existence of objects be pacified; you will also abide without any fixation on the subjective experiencer, and will rest in the nature of things, dharmata, which is a spacelike unity of clarity or lucidity and emptiness. Having realized it, to rest in that is the prajna paramita, the perfection of knowledge.

These last two perfections, the perfections of meditation and knowledge, correspond directly to the two qualities that develop in meditation practice, namely shamata and vipasyana. The fifth perfection, meditation, corresponds to shamata, and the sixth corresponds to vipasyana. Both of these, and especially prajna, are difficult to talk about and have to be experienced through gradual training and practice. However, the fact that they are difficult to talk about or difficult to understand merely through hearing about them does not mean they are impossible to realize. They can be realized by going through the stages of gradual training. It should be understood, though, that the manner of realization of these latter two does not arise through the acquisition of information, but it arises from within, through the power of your training. As was sung by Lord Marpa in one of his songs, "Even if all the buddhas of the three times were to appear to me, I would not have a single question to ask any one of them." When realization comes, it arises from within.

QUESTIONS AND ANSWERS

Question: I am still having difficulty understanding — on a practical level — being patient with the abuse of others. I can understand how projecting negativity onto others can feed into the situation and just make it worse, but in certain circumstances it seems really terrible to just sit by and watch abuse happen. It seems destructive to oneself, in a sense, to not take action. Could you say something about how to have the wisdom to understand when and how to practice patience properly? I understand it is important in some way to always practice patience. But what about, in the worst-case scenario, if somebody was being murdered in front of your eyes?

Rinpoche: First of all, the presentation here in a dharmic context is concerned with ultimately what we aspire to do, but it requires some adjustment to particular circumstances. We need to live in this world. In order to apply Dharma to our lives we need to use all of our intelligence in order to see how worldly circumstances and Dharma can work together.

The key point in response to your question is that practicing patience does not mean that no action should be taken. Being patient means that the action taken should not be motivated by anger. Therefore, whenever possible, you should be patient (in the sense of not becoming angry) when something negative is happening. If you cannot be patient, and you become angry, as soon as possible you should recognize that you have become angry and that you are being motivated by anger. You should understand that the way you act based on that anger may be problematic.

You have to commit yourself to not responding or reacting with anger to the abuse of others, but this does not mean that you should allow the abuse to occur. For example, if you see someone who is trying to kill someone (including yourself), the notion that you should be patient does not mean that you should allow the murder to occur. Whether it is you yourself that could be killed or someone else, that person would lose a precious human body for no good reason. As well, by allowing the killing to occur, you are allowing the killer to come to an unimaginable karmic disaster. Therefore, while in fact you should be patient in the sense of not getting angry, you should take steps to protect whomever is being threatened. This may be something you can do yourself, or it may involve enlisting the aid of someone else. In any case, there is no contradiction between protecting people from abuse and being patient with abuse.

We need always to be skillful in working with actual situations. Sometimes people have the misunderstanding that practicing patience means that you should allow someone to beat you up, kill you, or do any negative thing that they happen to think of. This is not right because, just as we ourselves have to observe the doctrine of karma and protect ourselves from doing negative things that will bring disaster on ourselves, in the same way we would want to protect others from this kind of situation as well. Therefore practicing patience does not mean allowing others to abuse you or anyone else.

Question: Could you speak about the wrathful aspect of compassion as expressed by some of the Tibetan deities? How that is connected with non-aggression?

Rinpoche: Deities can appear in different styles. Sometimes they are peaceful, sometimes they are wrathful, and sometimes they are semi-wrathful. A semi-wrathful deity is one that is a more or less peaceful deity with some expression of wrath. It is natural that we would wonder why there would be these different types or representations of deities. All of the forms that deities take are forms that are displayed with their particular characteristics in order to tame particular beings, which is in order to coincide with the aspirations and the makeup of particular beings. This essentially means that some people like peaceful deities. Then there are some that like wrathful deities, and some like semi-wrathful deities. The function of any of these three types of deities is identical. By relying upon a particular deity, the practitioner is able to reduce the kleshas and gradually eliminate them, and correspondingly expand his or her qualities and attain the common and supreme attainments. These deities appear in their particular forms in order to enable specific types of practitioners to progress in this accomplishment.

Ordinarily, we have a very naïve fixation on characteristics, and we take characteristics to represent some kind of inherent essence or nature in the thing that possesses those characteristics. Therefore when we see an iconographical representation of a peaceful deity, we think that the deity must represent some kind of really compassionate being. When we see a wrathful deity represented in iconography, we imagine that this must be a depiction of some kind of savage killer who has no compassion, and who is really furious, angry, and mean from the heart. This is incorrect. The appearance of deities in wrathful form is entirely because there are individuals who have more confidence in working with a deity who appears that way — who respond with more devotion than they would to a peaceful deity. However, all types of deities are equally a display of the same fundamental wisdom, and wrathful deities are not a depiction of the klesha of anger at all.

There is also a similar situation with respect to the depiction of male and female deities in sexual union. People often get the idea that this actually represents two beings who are somehow sexually united as they would be in mundane existence, but it actually has nothing whatsoever to do with this. The symbol is that the male deity represents the aspect of method or compassion, and the female deity represents the aspect of intelligence and knowledge, and the union between the two represents the unification of these otherwise disparate aspects of our development. It has nothing whatsoever to do with mundane sexuality.

It is very helpful to understand the reasons behind these aspects of iconography, both the iconography of peacefulness and wrath, and the iconography of male and female deities, and so on. For example, the protector Mahakala is shown in a particularly wrathful form. However, the liturgy of the Mahakala practice says, "Without wavering from the expanse of the dharmadhatu, you manifest within the dharmadhatu in a wrathful form as a protector." The meaning of this is that the particular form that deities such as the protectors manifest is the display of the wisdom of the dharmadhatu in a particular form that coincides with the appetite or faculties of particular practitioners. This iconography should not be misunderstood as the depiction or glorification of kleshas such as anger.

There is a further distinction that we need to understand between deities in general and wrathful deities in particular. There are two types of wrathful deities: wisdom deities and mundane deities. Wisdom deities are deities who abide upon any of the bodhisattva levels, from the first up to the tenth, and mundane deities are those who have not yet attained any of those levels. Thus there actually are mundane gods who are very, very powerful. Because they are not enlightened beings, there is the possibility that the power of these mundane deities could be misused, whereas the power of wisdom deities could not.

The Tibetans have a saying that "Gods, spirits, and humans are much the same." As we know, among human beings we will find people with different personalities, and in dealing with them you have to respect or be aware of their particular personal makeup. The meaning of the saying is that, in the same way, among spirits and among mundane gods, you will find different personalities, just as there are people who are particularly aggressive, or particularly jealous. In that same way you have to respect and be aware of the personality of the spirits and mundane gods you are dealing with.

Question: Could you say a bit more about what mundane deities are?

Rinpoche: Mundane deities are gods in the conventional sense, such as mountain gods, river gods, and so on, which actually do exist. These beings do play a certain role in things.

Question: In your discussion of the prajna paramita, the perfection of knowledge, you gave an eight-part analogy on the nature of illusion. The sixth one was the city of gandharvas, and I didn't understand that.

Rinpoche: The word gandharva means "smell eater." Gandharvas are beings who have only mental bodies, not flesh and blood bodies. They are nourished, or receive enjoyment, from smells. For example, beings in the bardo state are a type of gandharva. The analogy that was being given is to something that has no substantiality whatsoever.

There are gandharvas other than bardo beings as well, and they would probably be considered pretas if we were to fit them into the categories of the six realms. Some types of beings, by the way, can be categorized into more than one of the six realms. For example, very powerful, prosperous nagas are not generally classified as animals but are classified as gods, and the lesser, weaker nagas are classified as animals.

Question: How about the small beings, like gnome spirits, that live underneath the earth? Which category would they belong to? Are they spirits?

Rinpoche: It is hard for me to say about that. It probably depends on what they look like. If they look like little people, then probably we would have to include them in the human realm. If they look like little animals, then you would probably have to say they are in the animal realm. But I've never seen them so I can't tell you. Have you?

Something has to be said when we talk about gods and spirits. It is normal for human beings to imagine that these are very powerful beings, totally unlike ourselves. Certainly they normally exist in realms other than our own. However, whereas humans tend to regard spirits as very powerful and dangerous, spirits regard humans as very powerful and dangerous.

There is a story that is an illustration of this. At one time there was a man who befriended a spirit. The two of them were always going around together. One day they went for a very long journey, and in the midst of this journey they both got very hungry. The spirit said to the man, "Well, what are we going to eat? I'm famished." They looked up and they both saw a goat on the side of the mountain. The man said to the spirit, "Well, OK, either you go up, kill the goat, and I'll fetch water and make a fire so we can cook it, or I'll go up and kill the goat and you fetch water and make a fire so we can cook it." The spirit thought about it and said, "Well, fetching water and making a fire sounds like a lot of work, I'll go up and kill the goat." The spirit went up the mountainside, and the man set about making the fire and fetching the water and so on. Pretty soon he had the fire and everything all ready, and he was sitting by the fire sweating, waiting for the spirit to come back with the goat. He waited a very long time. Finally the spirit appeared, but without the goat. The man said, "Where's the goat?" The spirit said, "Well, I did not bring it yet." The man said, "Why not?" The spirit said, "Well, this is all going to take some time." The man asked, "What do you mean?" The spirit answered, "Well, I couldn't kill it on the spot. I'll tell you what I did. I put a very sharp stone in the crack in the goat's hoof, and it's going to get infected, and it's going to die, eventually." The man said to the spirit, "That's going to take ages! Never mind, I'll go up and kill it." So the man went up, killed the goat, and brought it back. And the spirit said to him, "Man, and they call *me* a demon!" The spirit was so frightened by what the human did that he ran away.

There are lots of minor spirits who really do not have much power, and who, because of their previous karma, are born in that particular realm and have a great deal of spite towards humans and so on. If they could do something harmful, they would do so, but there is not much they can do because they are rather weak. Normally we would not see them at all. However if you were someone who does see spirits, sometimes when you were trying to walk somewhere, a spirit would stand up and glare at you, and bite its lip in anger. But you would go right through it. It cannot really do anything to stop you.

Question: I have heard a Rinpoche say that it is better to have Mahakala as a protector, rather than the local or mundane deities. He said that it is all right to respect the mundane deities, but not to surrender to them because they are very possessive and they will do mischief in your life. Could you elaborate on that?

Rinpoche: That is true. In the Kagyu tradition, our major protectors are Mahakala (who is also called Gönpo Bernagchen), who is a bodhisattva residing on the tenth level, and Mahakali (also known as Palden Lhamo), who is a female bodhisattva abiding on the eighth level. The way that we traditionally relate to the protectors is that we view them as inseparable from our guru, and practice with them in that way. However, within the retinue of the protectors there are many mundane deities, and these mundane deities or lokapalas are fit to rely upon, because you are relating to them as being in the retinue of this wisdom deity. If you rely upon mundane deities independently of a wisdom deity, and especially if the particular mundane deity you are relying upon is one that is not particularly compassionate (which is not necessarily the case but may be the case) then there can be problems.

The relationship between the main wisdom deity and their mundane retinue is like the relationship between humans involved in this specific lineage. If we take our own Kagyu tradition as an example, there are many people who uphold and practice the Kagyu tradition, and among these people some are wisdom beings — bodhisattvas who have attained the bhumis such as His Holiness Gyalwa Karmapa and many others. However, by no means are all of us at that level. Most of us are still mundane beings. Thus we are somewhat like the mundane retinue surrounding the wisdom deity.

Question: Concerning the sixth paramita, prajna, is it a sort of cumulative development based on practicing the first five paramitas? Also, how does prajna relate to shunyata? Is shunyata the state of mind that happens with prajna?

Rinpoche: Actually, it is not so much the case that prajna is a result of practicing the first five paramitas as it is that prajna is an element that must be present in *all* of the paramitas. In an abbreviated presentation of the six paramitas such as we just had, we limit it to six, but in fact in a detailed analysis it is presented that each of the six has to contain all six. There is a generosity of generosity, a morality of generosity, and so on. Thus to actually *be* paramitas, to be perfections, there has to be an element of prajna always present in any of the others. Therefore it is not considered only a result.

The faculty of prajna is the means by which you realize shunyata. You could think of prajna as that faculty which brings about that realization. Thus the ultimate nature of things has to be realized by means of prajna.

Question: Are there many more spirits than human beings?

Rinpoche: In general the way it is taught is that among the six realms the beings who possess greater merit are fewer than those who possess less merit. Thus the less merit there is for beings in a particular realm, the more beings there will be in that realm. It is said that, for example, there are as many beings in the hells as particles in a large field, there are as many beings who are animals as grains of barley in a fermentation container, and there are as many gods or humans as there are motes of dust on your fingernail, and there are as many people with all the conditions for practicing the Dharma as stars you can see during the day. Because humans have more merit in general than spirits, it is fitting to say that there are more spirits than humans.

Question: I have another question on this topic. I have heard it taught that we have personal spirits. Are they like guides?

Rinpoche: Yes, there are all kinds of innate deities. There are innate mundane deities, which are gods with whom you are connected, such as the father god, mother god, ore god, hearth god, and life god. Then there are also innate wisdom deities, such as the forty-two peaceful deities who abide in your heart and the fifty-eight blazing wrathful ones who abide in your brain. Thus we have all kinds of deities who live in our bodies.

Naturally people are curious about all of this. No doubt it is fascinating to talk about things like the father god, mother god, uncle god, aunt god, and so on. But if you are trying to practice Dharma sincerely, it gets more in your way than it helps you, because you are trying to understand selflessness. If you think not only of yourself but also of all these extra beings, that makes all the more that you have to see through in the realization of selflessness.

Question: Concerning your explanation that each paramita contains all six paramitas, would it be a correct understanding that, for example, the prajna of generosity would be the culmination of that paramita?

Rinpoche: The prajna of generosity could be understood as having two aspects: mundane and supermundane. Supermundane prajna would be pure wisdom.

In the case of mundane knowledge or intelligence it is not really the culmination or outcome, because it is something that has to be present during the action for it to be a perfection. It would mean that while you are performing the specific act of generosity, you are not doing it casually, unconsciously, or carelessly. Instead you are bringing your full intelligence to bear on it, so that you are careful to give the thing, whatever it is, at a time and place and in a way that is appropriate, so that it will be beneficial. In other words, it is being conscious, and the prajna aspect is being free of any hope for some kind of personal payback, which would prevent it from being generosity. At that point the generosity is still mundane.

For true, supermundane generosity, there has to be a supermundane prajna, which is that recognition that the giver, the gift, and the recipient have no inherent existence. That same prajna, which is a freedom from conceptualization of the three elements of any virtuous action, would have to be present for the other four paramitas as well, for morality and so on.

Question: I have been thinking about the need for patience, and you have been explaining that each paramita needs to contain all the others. It would be helpful to understand just what the prajna of patience is.

Rinpoche: The prajna of patience is the intelligence that needs to take part in the correct application of patience in a specific situation. It applies to what we discussed in an earlier question about situations where, in the name of patience, someone might allow himself or herself to be abused. That is an example of what happens when you try to practice patience without prajna, without intelligence. Patience that is linked with prajna, that has the prajna of patience, would never become a naïve submission or masochism, because you would be very conscious of what act on your part would actually protect not only yourself but the other person in the best way. If you were aware, through using your prajna, that doing nothing was necessary, that there was no real danger in the situation and the degree of abuse was something you could put up with without any harm, then you would do nothing. You would be patient in the literal sense. If you were aware that it would be better to say or do something, or possibly that the situation was so dangerous that you needed to escape, you would do those things. You would not just stay there and subject yourself to it in the name of patience.

Question: I'm trying to understand what you mean by the idea that each of the paramitas contains the others. Would you say they are like levels of that paramita?

Rinpoche: You can think of them as levels if you want, but the point is that each of the six, to be authentic, has to have all these aspects. There is a discussion of this in the *Jewel Ornament of Liberation*, which gives an example of how one act, such as an act of giving something, contains the others. It explains the various aspects, showing that the giving itself is the generosity, and then there is patience involved in giving, and there is diligence involved in giving, and there is morality involved in giving, and so on. It shows how any virtuous action really has to have these six aspects.

Question: Can a virtuous action exist without all those aspects?

Rinpoche: It is possible that there could be a virtuous action that did not have aspects of the others. There could be a generosity without any kind of morality or ethics behind it, or there could be a kind of morality that was completely without any aspect of generosity. Obviously though, a virtuous action that is complete — one that has all six aspects — would be better.

There can also be actions that are wise and compassionate but that do not involve a conventional form of all six aspects we have discussed. For example in a previous life of the Buddha, he was the captain of a merchant vessel. He became aware that one of the passengers on the vessel was going to sink the vessel and kill all five hundred people on the ship. He realized that the only way he could stop the man was by killing him, so he did. It was an act of generosity because he saved the lives of the other passengers, and he also prevented that person from acquiring the karma of killing so many people. However, we could not call it an act of morality in the conventional sense.

On the other hand, it was an act of great prajna. In that lifetime the Buddha was a bodhisattva, and bodhisattvas do whatever is going to be of most benefit in any given situation. The choice that the captain was facing was either allow five hundred people to die, or kill one person. Implicit in the story is that there was no third alternative. He determined that if he killed this one person, then he would actually be benefiting him because he would be preventing him from killing five hundred people. If he did *not* kill him, he would obviously allow the five hundred people to be killed for no reason and allow that one person to cast himself into karmic disaster.

Question: This question is in regard to our discussion of spirits. Many of us in the West have grown up not particularly believing in them or being aware of them—at least not as much as I assume is the case in other cultures. Is there any point of view that you might have about how much attention we should give to spirits or not, and the effect that not paying attention to spirits might have? Does it matter?

Rinpoche: It is fine not to think about spirits at all; it makes no difference. When you are meditating on love and compassion, you can take the attitude, "May all beings without exception be benefited." You do not particularly have to itemize all the different kinds of beings. By saying "all beings" you are automatically embracing spirits and so on in your kindness. You do not have to think of them separately.

Question: In that story about the two monks, why were they terrified about the emptiness of all things?

Rinpoche: They were terrified because the two monks had what is known as a "shravaka disposition." There are five dispositions or potentials that are discussed in the mahayana Buddhist teachings. Sometimes these are called "families"

160

because they refer to groups or categories of people, specifically in relation to their propensities for Dharma. People naturally are born with, or grow up with, one of these particular types of disposition. Someone who is of a mahayana disposition will be naturally attracted to the mahayana view. Someone who is of a pratyekabuddha disposition will be drawn to that, and someone of a shravaka disposition will be drawn to that, and so on. The basic point is that when someone hears the doctrine of the emptiness of all things and delights in it, it indicates that they have a natural disposition to the mahayana. On the other hand, when someone whose predisposition is towards the shravakayana hears about the emptiness of all things, they will find it unsettling — to say the least.

This is why the Buddha's teaching was presented in the three sequential vehicles, which are the shravakayana, the pratyekabuddhayana, and the bodhisattvayana or mahayana. These were taught by him to correspond to the levels of acumen of the disciples — lesser, medium, and greater.

All three of these vehicles are paths that lead to full buddhahood. The difference is that in the case of the mahayana it is called a direct path, and the pratyekabuddhayana and the shravakayana are considered to be indirect or long paths.

Rinpoche's conclusion: Thank you, your questions have been good. It was said by the Buddha, "Bikshus, analyze my statements as you would refine gold ore." This means that we are taught not to accept anything uncritically, and not to simply hear something and then say, "Well, this is what the Buddha taught so we had better believe it without considering what it might actually mean." Therefore the question and answer process in studying the Dharma is as important as the lecture on which it is based. That is so because being able to understand what was said in the first place is based on individuals asking genuine questions and the others who are listening to those questions, and then all of us hearing the answers that come out in the discussion. Otherwise we tend to accept things uncritically, and without analyzing these statements, we tend not to understand all of their implications. Therefore, your questions are always helpful to other people and not just yourself.

Let us conclude by praying for the success of all worldly and Dharmic endeavors, and by dedicating the virtue of this teaching and all the virtue accumulated in the past, present, and future, to the unsurpassable happiness of all beings.

COLOPHON
The Special Benefit of Working for the Dharma and for the Activity of His Holiness the Gyalwa Karmapa

A Message to the KTD staff and community,
Karma Kagyu Sangha members,
& all those open to the blessings of His Holiness

In our present life situation, we have the good fortune to assemble here at this place known as Karma Triyana Dharmachakra, which was established by His Holiness the 16th Gyalwa Karmapa, Rangjung Rigpe Dorje, as his main seat in the West. Based on his having established this, and based on our involvement with the center, many of us actually work at and serve the center, and others may be members or friends of the center. In short, because of this involvement we have the opportunity to encounter all the teachers who come here, as well as to practice together.

If you understand the significance of your situation, you will see that having the opportunity to learn and understand the Dharma, and having the opportunity to assemble and practice together as we do, is extraordinarily rare. If you reflect upon this, you will come to understand that we possess a good opportunity and an obvious degree of merit that is quite uncommon in this world.

Exactly what is this opportunity that we have? It is the opportunity to actually cultivate and develop the bodhicittas of aspiration and implementation. These must be developed or cultivated — it is not just a matter of learning about or understanding these aspects of bodhicitta. We cannot simply generate bodhicitta by reading about it in a book, for example. In order to cultivate these bodhicittas, we have to go through the stages of training, the stages of practice or cultivation, that are the same as those that all the buddhas and bodhisattvas of the past have gone through. Therefore, without such an opportunity as this, it is impossible to cultivate them.

All of us are connected in our various ways and serve in various ways at Karma Triyana Dharmachakra, which was created by His Holiness the 16th Gyalwa Karmapa. We might ask exactly who the Karmapa is. The name "Karmapa" means a person who is the embodiment of activity or action. This refers to the actions, the power, and the blessing of all the buddhas of the past, all the buddhas of the present, and all the buddhas of the future. Thus the true significance of the name Karmapa is that he embodies in one person all the power and blessing of all buddhas. What exactly does this activity consist of? From the viewpoint of all the buddhas and bodhisattvas, the only thing that is to be done—the only activity that is to be engaged in—is the benefit of beings, and this chiefly means establishing all beings without exception in the state of permanent freedom and happiness. Since this is the fundamental intention or motivation, and is therefore the fundamental activity of all buddhas and bodhisattvas, then as the embodiment of all their activity, the Karmapa's activity consists entirely of benefiting others.

Furthermore, it is said in the Buddhist scriptures that the only way to please buddhas is to please beings. This means that aside from doing anything and everything that helps or pleases sentient beings, there is no other way to actually cause pleasure to a buddha. Making offerings to buddhas, praising buddhas, and so on does not directly please them. Therefore, since the only thing that is truly pleasing to buddhas is the benefiting of sentient beings, it is of great significance that we have the opportunity to do this.

How does this opportunity arise for us? The Karmapa is the embodiment of the activity of all buddhas of the past, present, and future. As for ourselves, we have taken birth as human beings, and a part of our makeup is that we fixate very strongly on self and other, and on all kinds of similar, related dualities. This means that for us to be able to meaningfully relate to a teacher, that teacher must manifest as a human being—otherwise we would be completely unable to relate to such a being. Therefore, although the Karmapa is completely liberated in that he is the embodiment of the activity of buddhas of the past, present, and future, he continually manifests as a human being, for otherwise we would have no way to contact him.

Anything we do that is done in service of the Dharma in fact becomes an aspect of, a part of, the Karmapa's activity. This means that even though we may lack the realization or constant compassion of the buddhas and bodhisattvas of the past, if we engage in all of our actions with the purest of motivations, then everything we do becomes the source of truly immeasurable merit. It has been said that since all things depend upon the mind, all outcomes depend upon motivation, and therefore the most important thing in choosing and engaging in any course of action is the motivation with which it is done.

When you are working for a Dharma center, it is important to maintain this pure motivation, and not to work there in order to try to acquire some kind of rank or position or power. We are following and supporting the work of the bodhisattvas of the lineage, and they never thought in terms of power or status. If you *do* think this way, it would not be much different than a mundane situation such as working for a big company, where people are just thinking about promotions, more status, and more pay.

The situation of working for the Dharma is one in which we could accumulate great merit. But if you bring an improper motivation to this opportunity, it is like taking that drop of water that is the merit you accumulate and swallowing it. At that point, it is lost.

What does it mean to have a pure motivation in the context of this tradition? It begins with the recognition that since we have acquired the eighteenfold precious human existence, we have the opportunity to do something that is useful not only for ourselves but also for others. On the basis of understanding that, pure motivation consists of generating the intention that everything you do will be beneficial to yourself and others. If you engage in your various activities such as serving or working for the center with that intention, and if you maintain as your basic motivation for doing so the desire to benefit yourself and others in a true way, and cast aside such ephemeral motivations as hoping for fame, or good reputation, prosperity, and so on, then as long as you maintain the good motivation, and act in a way that accords with the culture of this country and so on, then your work itself will become a cause of your generation of bodhicitta.

If you reflect upon the opportunity you possess, and if you reflect upon how extraordinary it is and how much merit there is in this opportunity, then you will have more enthusiasm and more interest in fulfilling your responsibilities and in other acts of service. I am mentioning this because this is the attitude I try to take myself. I feel that I am very fortunate and have great merit to be able to have this opportunity to serve the Karmapa.

The most important thing to remember in this community — and this also applies to human society at large — is that our situation is one in which many different people are living together. Since we are all human beings, and as human beings we all have kleshas, then there will be ups and downs in the community life. Sometimes you will be happy, sometimes you will be sad, sometimes there will be some shortcomings in your behavior, and sometimes not. In serving the activity of His Holiness, though, the basic thread that needs to run through all of these ups and downs is the recollection of your reason for being here. If you remember that as your fundamental motivation, which it obviously is, and that the Karmapa is the embodiment of all of the activity of the buddhas of the past, present, and future, then you will be able to be confident that everything you do with the proper motivation is assisting the Karmapa in his activity. In fact, we could even go further and say that everything you do that is done in service to the Karmapa is part of the Karmapa's activity. Since that is the case, then even though you may regard yourself as ordinary and not having much power, because His Holiness himself is the embodiment of the power and blessing of all buddhas and bodhisattvas – provided your motivation is pure – then everything you attempt to do will definitely without any doubt be effective.

There is an example of how working within the mandala of enlightened beings can be so profoundly effective, and it concerns the dedication of merit that we do at the end of practice or any virtuous activity. In doing the dedication of merit, we pray that the merit of such practice or activity be dedicated to the supreme enlightenment of all beings. However, as ordinary beings, we are not fully able to perform this act of dedication in a perfectly pure way. There is a way that we can make our dedication effective in spite of that. We can do so by recollecting the manner of dedication of all buddhas and bodhisattvas of the past. If you think, "Just as all buddhas and bodhisattvas of the past have dedicated all of their merit to the supreme happiness of all beings, in the same way I make that same dedication," then through the power of making reference to the perfect dedications made by buddhas and bodhisattvas, the dedication becomes effective. Doing the dedication in this way, it is as though our one drop of merit has been poured into the vast ocean of all the merit of all buddhas and bodhisattvas. It will never be exhausted as long as that ocean of vast merit is not dried up. In the same way, even though we recognize that we ourselves may not have any particular power or effectiveness to benefit beings, if we can continue to maintain a pure motivation in our actions of service, then we actually come to share in the Karmapa's activity. And through dedicating all of our merit accumulated in support of his activity in the way that was just described, then all of this becomes a source of truly immeasurable and inexhaustible merit.

The degree of merit you accumulate in a given action depends in large part upon the attitude with which you have done the action. Depending upon the attitude, the same action can cause either a vast or a very small amount of merit. For example, when the Buddha was alive, there were those who had great faith in him, those who had no faith in him, and all sorts of varieties of attitudes in between. This was because of the different karma and different merit of those various beings. The situation is exactly the same today. The nature of karma has not changed. Therefore, all of the different circumstances in which we find ourselves, as well as the different results of our actions, depend upon our attitudes.

However, in spite of the fact that beings, based upon their different attitudes, will accumulate different degrees of merit, this does not mean that buddhas and bodhisattvas have different attitudes towards those beings. Buddhas and bodhisattvas are free of any kind of preference. They do not think, "Well, this being has a great deal of faith in me and serves me well, so I will help them, and this being does not like me and in fact hates me so I will not help them." The compassion of buddhas and bodhisattvas is totally free of that kind of preference, and is much more like the way the sun shines in the sky. The sun is simply spontaneously present in the sky, and does not have to think, "Well, I'll shine tomorrow, but maybe I will not shine the next day." The sun also displays no partiality in terms of what it shines upon. It does not think, "These things are clean; I'll shine on them. These things are dirty; I will not shine on them," and so on. Just like that, the compassion of buddhas and bodhisattvas is extended equally for all beings.

Although the blessings of enlightened beings are always present, the degree of blessing we actually receive depends mainly on our own attitude. For example, in the case of the Karmapa, it is said that the Karmapa bestows liberation merely by being seen. This means literally that if you meet the Karmapa in person or see an image of the Karmapa such as a photograph, there is some kind of liberation that occurs. Now this does not mean that merely by seeing the Karmapa you will attain the bodhisattva levels immediately. It means that anyone who sees the Karmapa has a seed of their future liberation planted within them. This is especially true, of course, if you are delighted in the Karmapa, if you have great faith in the Karmapa, and so on. But even if you merely view the Karmapa as some kind of mundane celebrity, or even if you were to actually dislike the Karmapa, the seed of liberation would still be planted. This is also true with regard to his speech, which is said to bestow liberation upon being heard. This does not mean that merely by hearing the Karmapa speak you will attain liberation on the spot, but just as when you see him, the seed of your future liberation is planted.

Since the seed of liberation is planted in any case, we might ask what the distinction is between the seed that is planted when, for example, someone sees the Karmapa with an attitude of great faith, and when someone sees the Karmapa with a negative attitude, of actually disliking him. The distinction lies in the speed with which liberation will be attained. The process begins with seeing the Karmapa, and the process culminates in the liberation of that person. If the person who sees the Karmapa has a pure motivation, makes good aspirations, and in general has great faith, then there will be a comparatively short amount of time in between their seeing the Karmapa and their attaining liberation. If, on the other hand, the person who sees the Karmapa reacts to the Karmapa with aversion or dislike, then while the seed of liberation is still definitely planted within them, the period of time it will take for them to become liberated will be much longer.

It is said of bodhisattvas in general that a positive connection with them bestows buddhahood in one life, and a negative connection with them will at least end samsara. This means that you will not wander in samsara forever, but at some point it will come to have an end for you. Thus any connection with buddhas and bodhisattvas is of course beneficial, but the best and most beneficial kind of connection

169

is a connection based upon a good attitude on your part, such as faith. The very best situation is a connection that is entered into with the intention of bodhicitta. In this way we all have this extraordinary opportunity at the present time.

The Karmapa manifests in a way that is like a lotus flower. Although the lotus grows out of the mud, when it blooms it has no mud in its bloom but is completely beautiful and perfect and pure. The Karmapa is the embodiment of the activity of all buddhas of the three times, but in order to actually benefit beings, he has to appear in ways that we can perceive him, in particular as a human being. He has done this again and again, and although he continues to appear as a human being, he does not do so out of kleshas that are out of control, as is the case with ordinary beings. However, to say that he is free of kleshas does not mean that he cannot exhibit joy and sadness. It is merely saying that he does not get out of control. As ordinary beings, when we experience joy, we are so intoxicated or overcome by it that we lose all sense of perspective and are completely out of control. That does not happen to the Karmapa. Also, when we get upset about something, we lose our tempers, and completely get out of control, and that does not happen to him either.

The reason this needs to be mentioned is that simply saying that he is free from kleshas might lead to a misunderstanding. We might think that the Karmapa is completely insensitive and numb, that he experiences no joy and sadness. This is not true—he is extraordinarily sensitive. He is the embodiment of the compassion of all buddhas of the three times, and through that compassion he is born again and again, and is prepared to do anything he has to do to benefit beings, such as giving up his own life, possessions, and so on. He has extraordinary awareness as well. For example, we know fairly well what has happened to us today, but we have no idea what is going to happen to us tomorrow. This is not the case with the Karmapa. Going back to his lifetime as the First Karmapa, he was given the name "One who knows all throughout the three times." This is because for a very long time he has had the ability to clearly see not only the present, but the past and the future, like something placed in the palm of his hand. Someone who can see the future and the past as clearly as the present could hardly be called insensitive.

It is said that if the intention or motivation is good, then the progress on the path will be good. If the intention is poor, then the progress on the path will be poor. Thus the most important factor in our training and in our lives is preserving a good motivation, and in order to do that, we need to remind ourselves of the opportunity we have. First of all, we have been born as human beings, and beyond that we have actually met the genuine teachings of Dharma. And most especially, we have the opportunity to serve His Holiness the Karmapa, who is the embodiment of the activity of all the buddhas of the three times.

News and information about Ven. Bardor Tulku Rinpoche's teachings and activities can be found at **www.kagyu.org**, the site of Karma Triyana Dharmachakra Monastery (KTD). KTD is the Western seat of His Holiness Ogyen Trinley Dorje, the 17th Gyalwa Karmapa. See also **www.raktrul.org**, the site of the Raktrul Foundation, an organization founded by Bardor Tulku Rinpoche to benefit his home monastery in Eastern Tibet and to continue its unique teachings.

Also by Bardor Tulku Rinpoche from Rinchen Publications:

The Practice of Green Tara
A Teaching on the Tashi Prayer
The Kagyu Lineage and the Activity
 of the Karmapas
Rest for the Fortunate — The Extraordinary Practice of
 Nyungne: Its History, Meaning, and Benefits